Praise for *Free to Fly*

"Parents everywhere are struggling with decisions around tech, including me. Fortunately, we have passionate experts like Nicole Runyon to guide us. This is why Nicole was one of the first people I reached out to when launching the Scrolling 2 Death podcast. *Free to Fly* is an important guide in a societal shift from 'the anxious generation' to a generation of strong, independent and healthy kids."

—NICKI REISBERG, Founder and Host of Scrolling 2
Death Podcast

"*Free to Fly* comes out swinging at a culture overflowing with diagnoses. Its surprises will open many minds—and many childhoods."

—LENORE SKENAZY, Author of *Free-Range Kids*

"Nicole Runyon offers practical advice and heartfelt encouragement to help parents raise confident, independent kids. *Free to Fly* is a relatable and inspiring guide for today's families."

—HANNAH OERTEL, Founder of Delay Smartphones

"A compelling book that explains why so many kids are failing to thrive—and what parents can do about it. Nicole Runyon writes with compassion, urging parents to show up for their kids. She gives them permission to say no, which just might be the most important thing they'll ever hear."

—KATHERINE JOHNSON MARTINKO, Author of *Childhood Unplugged: Practical Advice to Get Kids Off Screens and Find Balance* and *The Analog Family* Substack Newsletter

"Every parent-to-be, parent, and educator must read this book—now! Too many children today are struggling with poor mental health because adults have failed to teach them how to develop age-appropriate courage, independence, and resilience—both physically and mentally. Instead, many children are in therapy, where they're often labeled, encouraged to blame others for their feelings, and prescribed medications to numb their discomfort. We've never lived in a more complex society, which includes—but isn't limited to—overwhelming tech immersion and nutrient-deficient diets, so children today face unique challenges. If future generations are going to thrive, adults must step up and provide the guidance and support children need to develop healthy, resilient brains. Thankfully, this experienced and wise therapist (and now author) has created a simple, evidence-based road map to help adults prepare children to thrive!"

—DELIA MCCABE, PhD, Former
Psychologist-turned-Neuroscientist

"Any parent who is searching for answers needs to read *Free to Fly* by Nicole Runyon. After twenty-one years of working with families she has learned what we need to raise healthy kids. She shares her personal story of what has happened to our culture and how it's not too late to change things. When we think of how much technology has impacted the mental health of our kids, then we need to look for solutions. These solutions are in this book. What's more important to the life of your children than investing in this information? I only wish I'd had this book when I was raising my own kids fifteen years ago."

—LESLIE WEIRICH, Mental Health Speaker, Author of *The Gifts of Grief: How Four Decades of Loss Shaped My Life*

"This book is an absolute treasure and is crucial for this generation and those to follow. There is simply nothing else out there as informative, current, and accessible. I am eager to get *Free to Fly* into the hands of all the parents and teens I work with."

—MIRIAM MANDEL, MD, Pediatrician and Teen Coach

Free to Fly

Free to Fly

THE SECRET TO FOSTERING INDEPENDENCE IN THE NEXT GENERATION

NICOLE RUNYON, LMSW

Published by Mission Driven Press, an imprint of Forefront Books, Nashville, Tennessee.
Distributed by Simon & Schuster.

Library of Congress Control Number: 2024927038

Print ISBN: 978-1-63763-377-9
E-book ISBN: 978-1-63763-378-6

Cover Design by Studio Gearbox
Interior Design by Bill Kersey, KerseyGraphics

Printed in the United States of America

Dedication

For Oliver and Noelle, all I ever wanted was to be a good mom to you. This is for you and for all children whose parents want the same.

CONTENTS

INTRODUCTION

I ATTENDED A WORKSHOP AT MY SON'S HIGH SCHOOL about today's children and the mental illness epidemic we are experiencing. There was talk about technology and how it affects mental health. Talk about who is influencing our kids and the mental health decline. The content was educational for parents. There was audience discussion about how it was when we were kids: more outdoor play, independence, pick-up games, and parents didn't have to oversee their kids' schedules. It all sounded much like nostalgia. Not many solutions.

When it came time to talk about solutions, I found the approach to be lacking. The message was too soft. Let the kids have their devices; put parental controls on them even if the kids can circumvent. At least you are doing something. Then several references to how parents should just drink their sorrows away to cope with what's happening to our children.

Cheap jokes to get audience laughter.

I didn't find it funny.

If this is what psychologists have to offer parents, then we are doomed. We have real problems, and we need strong adults to help our children with those problems. The children are not all right. We can't ignore, surrender, drink, binge-watch TV, mindlessly scroll, and otherwise bury our heads in the sand.

Come on, adults, we can do better than this!

We have heard it countless times: We are experiencing a mental health epidemic with our children. I don't consider it a mental health problem though. I think it's a cultural problem. The culture is causing the mental health symptoms. In the age of digital connectivity, today's youth, often referred to as "screenagers," find themselves immersed in a world dominated by screens and electronic devices. Pew Research statistics in 2014 and 2015 indicate that the average teen sends a staggering sixty texts per day, while eight- to eighteen-year-olds spend an average of six hours daily in front of screens. When factoring in multitasking—juggling multiple devices simultaneously—this figure escalates to an astonishing seven and a half hours.[1]

To find a solution to this problem, I decided to transition from being a child psychotherapist to a speaker, author, and parent coach. As I made this change, an old memory resurfaced. I recalled the moment my childhood pediatrician announced his retirement. Reflecting on the shift in medical practices, he remarked, "I used to be the most important person in the office, but now it's the person handling insurance billing." His observation underscored the encroachment of HMOs in healthcare. The news deeply affected my mother, who was his patient and had then entrusted him with the care of her five children.

As I thought of this, I couldn't help but notice the parallels to my experiences with child psychotherapy. Nowadays, diagnosing, labeling, and pathologizing children are prerequisites for treatment coverage, despite the underlying environmental factors contributing to their issues. Insurance-coverage issues and documenting seem to take up more time than seeing the children. The most important thing is no longer the child.

Then there was the issue that I was becoming the most important person in the room. For a therapist, if we are the most important person in the room, something is wrong. I began to receive praise for being a therapist. The major mental health decline was upon us. My answer to the question "What do you do?" received rave reviews, as if I had invented the cure for cancer. I was perplexed. I had been a therapist for many years at that point and had never gotten such reception. I was also not feeling good about that praise. Therapists aren't supposed to be looked upon as saviors; we are supposed to help people save themselves. It was disconcerting that I was being treated like a hero. I didn't like it.

That was the beginning of my transformation.

Therapists are the mirror, the reflection and nothing else. We are meant to hold space for our clients. Holding space means you sit in someone's pain with them. You don't offer platitudes to make them feel better or try to solve their problem. Sometimes it means saying nothing and experiencing a therapeutic silence; other times it's showing them you are actively listening by reflecting back to them something they said. By being silent or reflecting to them what they are experiencing, you give them the opportunity to sit in their pain, not avoid it. You wait for them to figure out what they want to do.

If you have food in your teeth and you don't know and no one tells you, you will likely go through your day never being the wiser. It may cause you embarrassment, but you won't know it because no one will say it to your face. However, eventually if that food stays in your teeth and you never look in the mirror or brush your teeth, it will cause you problems. Most people come to therapy when the "food" they have been ignoring because they haven't looked at it is causing problems. It's not a therapist's job to tell them what is in their teeth. It's a therapist's job to ask, essentially, "Have you looked in the mirror lately? If not, you really ought to." When they look in the mirror, they see what they have been avoiding and this can be painful. Therapists sit in the pain with our clients and through this connection, change can begin.

When clients do, they see the food, they can figure out what to do about it because now they've seen it. They can floss, brush, use a toothpick, a water flosser, a floss stick, or, if the food is *really* lodged, they can go to the dentist to get the food removed. It's not a therapist's job to tell them which tool to use, only to help them identify the problem and then hold space for what they want to do about it. We are not the heroes in the story. The individual is. The one who decided to look in the mirror and see the problem. That is the hard work.

Bearing witness to this process was a gift for me. One that I was grateful for every day. I loved my work. I felt honored that anyone would trust me to be that person for them. Especially parents trusting me with their children. The one to sit in the room with them. I loved it and felt like I could do it forever.

Until I couldn't.

I was starting not to love it. I thought that was temporary. Perhaps it was compassion fatigue, burnout, chronic stress. I took more time off, stopped seeing patients within insurance networks to reduce my administrative tasks, raised my prices, and focused on my health. I thought that would do it. Still, I felt something was not right. Then, I realized what I had known for a long time.

It's not the kids; it's the parents.

I estimated 70 percent of my child psychotherapy practice were kids whose *parents* needed coaching, and the remaining 30 percent were kids who needed therapy. In her book *Bad Therapy: Why the Kids Aren't Growing Up*, Abigail Shrier highlights this growing issue of putting children in therapy who don't need it.[2]

This book is written for the 70 percent of parents who think that therapy is going to help their child. I am here to tell you it won't. I did this work and have been a psychotherapist for twenty-one years. The 30 percent of kids who need therapy can't get it because the others are taking up space in therapists' offices. The 70 percent don't get better; in fact, in most cases they get worse, so they occupy space for longer. Once I recognized this, I began to make changes to my practice. Changes that allowed children to get relief from their symptoms faster and for parents to feel more in control. Children no longer felt something was wrong with them.

Instead of seeing children for therapy, I began working with parents. Sometimes parents need coaching, other times they need therapy themselves. I was able to meet them where they were in their process and in the family dynamic. I found that working with parents helps children get better faster. I help children through helping their parents. Parents, you are the leaders of your family. If you are healthy, your children will be healthy.

One of the first families I worked with in this way responded well. I saw the two oldest siblings for therapy twice. Collectively, I could have diagnosed these children with attention deficit disorder, oppositional defiant disorder (has no respect for parental authority or boundaries), obsessive compulsive disorder, anxiety, and screen addiction. These children were reacting to their parents' stress and lack of coping skills to manage it. Their behaviors were the result of subconscious desire to gain control in an environment that didn't feel under control. Their parents lacked a united front. They agreed on the rules and boundaries, but one of them was not enforcing the rules. The children saw this fracture and used it to their advantage, manipulating the parents to get what they wanted. Each time this rendered the parents frustrated and overwhelmed, preventing them from continuing to enforce rules out of their own exhaustion.

The children's mother accompanied them to the sessions each time, and rather than diagnosing the children, I planted some seeds with their mother about my thoughts on their family dynamic and how it was affecting the children's behavior. By the end of the second session their mother said, "So it's not the kids, it's us; I think we need to come in." The parents worked on themselves individually, then on their marriage, making it more solid. This resulted in consistent parenting and mutually agreed-upon rules and boundaries. The children responded well to their parents' working on themselves, and their behaviors changed. One of the siblings went from having screaming fits for hours at bedtime, rendering the entire house exhausted from a lack of sleep, to going to bed peacefully with a simple bedtime routine and a tuck-in from Mom and Dad.

Abigail Shrier talks about a phenomenon called "iatrogenesis," in which the healer makes things worse. An example of this are kids who exhibit severe mental health issues because their parents want to be their "friend" and make them happy and comfortable all the time. In these pages, I will discuss why this and other factors are at the root of so many psychological disorders in children. Therapy can make these issues worse because the child ruminates about their feelings and themselves. They aren't made to be uncomfortable and work through hard things, necessary childhood tasks that have more benefits than you can imagine.[3]

By the end of this book, you will be able to recognize if your child needs therapy, or if you as the parent need to make changes to the landscape so your child can not only heal from issues they are struggling with but also gain a sense of self-trust and agency. I am trained to see the child in the context of their environment. We must look at the culture in which today's children are being raised if we want to find answers for how to help them. I've been in the minds of your children for more than two decades; I want you to know what I know so you can help them.

I had been practicing for thirteen years when I started my journey to find out what was happening. I had recently started specializing in adolescent and teen girls. I fell into that specialty because I got so many calls from parents of girls in middle and high school that my entire practice became full of those patients. I thought I would be doing some parent-child conflict resolution, issues I had learned about in my education and through my practice that are typical to the population. What I thought I knew for sure was that I was going to be working with teens and their families.

I was trained in family systems theory, which is essentially the idea that each member of the family has their role. Often, the identified patient in therapy is the "problem child" whom the family views as needing to be fixed. The parents see the therapist as the "fixer." This scenario cuts the parent out of the treatment and puts the responsibility of healing the family dynamic on the child. This is wrong, and much too big of a burden to bear for a child. What we clinicians know is that a family often does not even know that each individual has a role in the "problem." Therapy is meant to help with that understanding, and so working with children for me has always meant working with their families. At this point in my career, I had a lot of experience with this population.

However, I was finding family systems did not apply. All the things I thought I knew were out the window. I was blown away! After doing psychosocial histories and interviewing the adolescents with their families, I found something entirely different to be true. My certainty that I knew how to help a struggling adolescent was beginning to wane. I was finding that the families were intact and had good communication. There were things to work on, don't get me wrong, but not enough was going on in the family to warrant the symptoms the teens were presenting with. What I noticed was a pattern, a pattern I could trace to one common denominator at the time: screens.

I later learned that it wasn't just digital technology causing the mental illness epidemic, it was parents eroding their children's independence and developmental need for discomfort; body inflammation from lack of proper nutrition; physical, cognitive, emotional, and spiritual development stunted because of children not getting what they need from their environments; and children not learning basic skills for life, rendering them dysfunctional in the real world.

I began speaking to parent groups at schools and community organizations. Sounding the alarm to what I thought technology was doing to this generation of children. It was 2016. People were interested in the message, but not in making any changes. At the time technology was being celebrated and encouraged for children. It wouldn't be until recently, after the isolation and overuse of tech during the lockdowns, that the mental illness epidemic would reach a breaking point.

In response to the effects of lockdowns in 2020, I made a change. A revolutionary one. One that has proved to help more families. One where children get better by proxy, through their parents. Quickly. No therapy. No medication. Parents feel more control. Kids grow to be healthy and confident.

I don't diagnose anymore. I don't diagnose because I don't focus on the symptoms or the pathology. Call it what you like, but we must stop with the letters. ADD/ADHD, GAD (generalized anxiety disorder), MDD (major depressive disorder), OCD (obsessive-compulsive disorder), ODD (oppositional defiant disorder). Put a label on it. It doesn't matter what letter you attach to it. The symptoms are telling us a story.

I focus on the story. The story of a child who doesn't turn in his assignments (ADD). The story of a teenager who self-harms (such as cutting, a maladaptive way to avoid depressive feelings). The story of a child who doesn't listen and is constantly misbehaving (ODD). All of these are a result of something else going on deep down inside. I dig deep. That's what I do.

The story is my "why," my purpose in writing this book. To share my message with today's parents. You have more power than you think. Your kids don't have to struggle with their mental health.

A profound exploration of the issue is imperative, pinpointing the fundamental triggers behind the mental illness crisis.

The answer lies within the family unit—a proactive approach that involves equipping children with early coping mechanisms, fostering resilience, and promoting development devoid of excessive technology.

Empowering parents with the necessary tools to navigate the challenges posed by a technology-saturated culture is pivotal. By comprehending the evolutionary journey that has led us to this point, we can reshape the landscape for the current generation.

It's time to extricate technology from education, family dynamics, and the social lives of our children. Safeguarding their formative years is our key to averting the alarming surge in mental health complications that we presently face.

ADD/ADHD is a way for children to disconnect from painful feelings. If they don't like something, if something is too hard, if they have had trauma. Their brains are powerful and sophisticated. We can train our brains to go somewhere else, not to be present, not to focus or remember. ADD/ADHD is just a set of symptoms telling us something. Add technology to a child's life who already disconnects, and you'll see severe ADD.

Have you ever seen a deer in a car's headlights? Notice how the deer shakes? They are shaking out the trauma. Humans don't do that. Humans have the capacity to dissociate from trauma so we can function. It's survival. It's necessary so we can react in the moment and not freeze like a deer. The problem lies in not processing the trauma and instead developing maladaptive ways to manage it. Many check out and display ADD symptoms.

What happens then? Referral to therapy and a psychiatrist, only to feel more shame that there is something wrong. A pathology. Treating the symptoms. When really the symptoms are very explainable and can be worked out.

Simple, but not easy. Children are sensitive to their environments. I have learned in the twenty-plus years I've been doing this work that there are many reasons why children are reacting the way they are.

Aren't we taking the easy way out when we slap a diagnosis on them, send them to therapy, and put them on medications without more digging and figuring out the underlying causes for their ailments? Our children deserve so much more. There are those in my field would have you believe a diagnosis is permanent. By using words such as "neurodivergent" they are implying there is no way out. It's just how your brain works. Many kids in this category are given digital devices to "calm" them. Kids with diagnoses such as anxiety disorder, ADHD, and OCD are in this category. Before insurance coverage for mental health services, we saw these diagnoses as changeable. They were never meant to be permanent. They were meant to look at a set of symptoms and treat the root cause, not the symptoms. We used to do short-term therapy to work through anxiety and teach organizational skills for ADHD rather than immediately refer children to psychiatry for medication. I never treat anyone as if they are powerless. There are no victims. All children and parents can do the hard work.

Many therapists tell parents the device is the child's "lifeline." I call that giving up! It's not their lifeline. Kids with autism, for example, are already locked into themselves; why would you give them a device to lock them in further? When I learned about how to treat autism I studied a concept from The PLAY Project founded by Dr. Richard Solomon. The premise is that you engage with the child in any way you can. He calls it *open circles*: If you can get eye contact through play, you open them up to the world. It is so beautiful. I worked with kids with autism in this way before private practice. I didn't get many autism referrals in private practice because my level of care wasn't enough for them. Years later I'm now hearing therapists talk about giving kids with autism smart devices to calm them. I am baffled at this.

One of the most disturbing effects I've witnessed of pathologizing children is they begin to see themselves as powerless to their diagnosis. They wear the label as if it defines them. They use it as a crutch to avoid having to work through adversity. A diagnosis is an explanation, not an excuse. Not an excuse to get out of class to go to the "chill room" at school, or not be expected to be responsible for yourself or take care of your basic needs. The answer isn't to continue to give kids an out from doing something they don't want to do. Chill rooms in schools are merely a way for kids to avoid having to be challenged. School counseling offices are often filled with kids who want to sit there for long periods to avoid having to be in class. We must stop allowing kids to be victim to a diagnosis. "She has depression, so she can't clean her room" or "He has anxiety, so he needs testing accommodations" is not the way to help our children grow. They must work through those symptoms of depression and anxiety and come out the other side feeling strong and capable.

There is no script in this book. Plenty of so-called parenting experts give scripts for exactly what to say to kids in what moment. I think there is a time and a place for parents to learn what to say, but it should come from you, from a connected place. That requires you, the parent, to do a lot of work, because you are the expert for your child. You know what they need more than anyone. Parents have power. Don't ever let anyone tell you differently. Not even me! I'm not here to tell you what to do. I'm here to teach you about what kids need, when they need it, and how to work through your discomfort of separating from them.

I want you to feel ready to work through your emotional blocks. Self-reflect and ask yourself what is in the way of allowing your child to go through the pain that is growing up, so you can allow your child to be free to fly.

Extras

If you haven't already, be sure to download the *Free to Fly Kit* by going to the website https://nicole-runyon.myka-jabi.com/-bonus-material or scanning the QR code below.

There, you will find hidden bonuses. Simply enter your name and email to receive the kit. The kit is tailored to help solidify what you learn about child development and technology's effects on development. You will embark on two assessments called *What Is Your Relationship with Technology?* and *How Independent Are Your Children?* These assessments are crafted to help you bring awareness to your use of digital technology and how it affects your family, as well as your ability to allow your children to do the tasks of development and grow to be thriving young adults. Lastly, there is an *Activities Cheat Sheet*, a list of age-appropriate activities you can do with your child as well as a list of activities your child can do on their own.

CHAPTER 1

THE MIRROR

*Your child's struggles mirror
your childhood struggles.*
—Nicole Runyon

Think about what makes you most upset when it comes to your child or children. What really fires you up? What causes you lose your cool? For me, it's when they leave a mess and have no intention of cleaning it up. When this happens, I must muster up *all* patience and ask nicely. I'm not perfect, so that doesn't always happen, but I am aware of what lights me up and why. I admittedly have yelled at my kids for not doing what I asked. This comes from my own immaturity. The part of myself that knows how to express and communicate my feelings effectively was underdeveloped. According to John Delony, counselor and mental health expert, "The only thing yelling at a kid does is show them what an immature, power hungry, out of control brat you are."[4] Harsh, but true. Your childhood underdevelopment will manifest in the way you feel about your child.

Now think about yourself. Do you see that same quality in you? Maybe you don't, but if you thought about it, you would recognize that what you see in your children that you don't like is exactly what you don't like about yourself. When my kids leave a mess, it makes me feel not seen and not heard. They don't mean to send me that message; it's the way I'm receiving it. So, here's the mirror. My subconscious screams, *Who do you think you are? How dare you leave this mess! I would never have imagined doing this when I was your age.* I would never have entertained the idea of leaving a mess I made for anyone else to clean up but me, and not only did I clean up after myself, I also cleaned up after my brothers. I told myself I was being the good girl, but it didn't feel good. I resented it and was angry. I often tried to avoid this part of myself because my anger was never met well. I didn't know how to communicate it effectively in my childhood, and the adults in my life didn't know how to help me. I did really well at avoiding. It's the reason I became a therapist for children; it shaped me, and I was successful at it. It worked. Until it didn't. When I became a mother, I had to face myself. Parenthood requires us to have a cold, hard look in the mirror. Our children are mini versions of us—and not just in the way they look like us. They mimic us. I could see my own reflection in my children's behavior.

I had adopted the archetype of the "good girl" since very early in my childhood. If I did things to please the adults in my life, then I received positive attention and praise, and this encouraged me to continue to engage in that behavior. I helped my mom with my younger siblings and household chores without being asked to minimize her stress. I was friendly and kind to my peers in school, which won the praise of my teachers, and I was a diligent and good student. I followed most of the rules when they made sense. Chewing gum didn't; I often got in trouble for that one! My siblings were all scholar athletes and won awards for their efforts. Not me, I won the award for good citizenship. I didn't know why at the time. I was just being myself. Being nice was how I defined myself, it was my entire self-worth. Later, I learned they gave me the award because I had stood up for a boy who was relentlessly bullied.

Like many girls, I was afraid to disappoint anyone. The first thing I discovered about myself in my own therapy was the unique way I avoided my feelings of discomfort. "You hide in the help," my therapist said. Until then, I hadn't known I was hiding. If I was helping and caretaking, I had value; that felt good. I thought I was angry because of some flaw in me, not because I wasn't learning how to work through discomfort. I was hiding because I didn't know there was a way out.

Being a helper materialized when I was eight years old. I grew up in a family with five kids. My brother was the oldest; I was second, thirteen months younger. Another brother was sixteen months younger, followed by my sister four years younger, and finally the baby of the family, a brother born when I was almost nine. My first memory of taking care of him was the day he and my mother came home from the hospital. He was crying in his bassinet, and my mom wasn't available to pick him up. I instinctually went to him, cradled him in my arms, and rocked him until he calmed. I remember being so proud of myself. My mom was proud of me, too, and grateful. Prior to this moment I didn't feel like I stood out, lost in a big family. I had finally found something I was good at, and it was a way for me to gain attention among the chaos of so many kids. That was the beginning of defining myself as a helper and caretaker.

As my kids grew and got closer to the age I was when my youngest brother was born, I found myself saying "when I was your age" statements. I would see a mess or some irresponsibility on their part, and I would lecture them. Like a mantra I would say, "When I was your age, I was changing Uncle Jason's diapers." What I should have said is, "I get really frustrated when you don't do what I ask. My frustration is mine, and it's for me to work out. Can we work on you doing what is expected of you because you are required to do chores in this family?"

I wasn't able to parent the way my children needed me to because what I didn't know then, but do know now, is that I was making the choice to be the good girl. No one put me in that role but me. I felt trapped in it, but I knew I had a part. I had burned myself out trying to please even after

I was aware of my "hiding in the help." I put myself behind bars, and I always had the key to free myself. I struggled with boundaries. It was always so uncomfortable for me to make them and keep them. My kids taught me how to have boundaries and keep them. I recognized they needed that from me, and I worked through my discomfort so I could be what they needed.

> **Discomfort is an indicator that your children are learning something you never had the chance to learn.**

On their end, they are being children. Children are self-centered until you teach them how to be responsible for themselves. Only then can they have respect for themselves, and that trickles down to having respect for others. That happens all along the way in their development, age appropriately, and will be explained in detail in the next chapter. It's a parent's job to know what their kids need developmentally and, despite the difficulty, to provide it for them.

Furthermore, not only are children a mirror for our own wounds, but the mirror tends to show up at the same ages we were when things didn't go so well in our childhoods. When you are emotionally lit up by your child's behavior or emotions, it's likely because at that exact age you have holes in your development. Something didn't go right for you, and it never got resolved. Do your three-year-old's meltdowns make you want to scream? Do you get angry with your nine-year-old for not picking up his socks? Does it make you feel crazy that your teenager is not more independent? All scenarios are likely because, respectively, your meltdowns weren't met well, you were expected to do more than was age-appropriate at nine, and perhaps you were neglected as a teenager.

> **Human nature is like water. It takes the shape of its container.**
> —*Wallace Stevens*

Emotion is energy. There is an energy transfer between child and parent in our interactions. Parents hold the space and act as the metaphorical "container" for their children; if this happens, children can be themselves. The parent container is the person or vessel that holds their child's emotion or energy. Imagine one hundred tennis balls bouncing around in a small room. Chaos, right? Think of the tennis balls as your child's feelings on any given day or in any given moment. Your job is to wrap your arms around those tennis balls to contain them. Not scoot them out of the room, rendering them gone and out of sight, problem solved. Contain the chaos. Once it's contained, they can decide what they want to do about it.

How do you contain it in real-world application? You show up, you listen, you support, and then you say, "What are you going to do about it? What is your part?" Kids usually don't like this; they want you to agree with them even when they are wrong and tell them they are right. But eventually they will appreciate you for not impeding on their autonomy and growth.

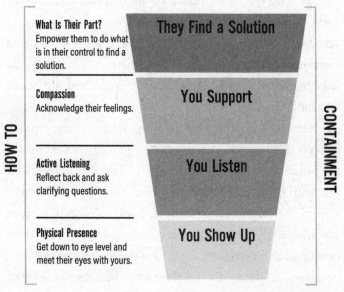

HOW TO

What Is Their Part?
Empower them to do what is in their control to find a solution.

They Find a Solution

Compassion
Acknowledge their feelings.

You Support

Active Listening
Reflect back and ask clarifying questions.

You Listen

Physical Presence
Get down to eye level and meet their eyes with yours.

You Show Up

CONTAINMENT

Source: Nicole Runyon

To show up physically, you sit next to them while they talk and offer to be close if they need that from you. Your facial expression and body language are important so you can show them you care. If you're standing, bend or stoop down to get on their level. Once your physical presence is clear, you listen. Listening requires you to hear what they are saying. Be sure not to interrupt. You can repeat their words in your own way and ask them if you have it right, so you understand what they are saying; this is called *reflecting back*. Ask open-ended questions to clarify their feelings. Then you support them by providing emotional support. Offer encouraging words and compassion. Don't misinterpret this as blanket validation. Their feelings are always valid but their reactions and actions aren't, necessarily. You can support feelings and correct behavior at the same time. Containment helps calm the nervous system. When a child's nervous system is calm, they can use their critical thinking skills, rationale, and judgment to problem-solve.

Parents, I know you want to fix it. Resist the temptation to tell your child what to do. Taking ownership for the solution is part of growing up. You can help talk it out with them by asking questions, but they must find a way to the other side of their difficult feelings. Children are ultimately responsible for how they manage their emotions and reactions. If you are the container, they can be successful doing that on their own once they've learned how to do so with your guidance and support.

Energy isn't what is said or done, it's covert. It's the space in between the parent and child. If a parent says something and doesn't have the energy needed behind their statement, the child will pick up on the energy, not the parent's words or actions. Being the container is hard work. It requires you to reflect on yourself and manage your emotions. Children are better at picking up on energy than adults as they are inherently more connected than adults. They are naturally intuitive. Today's children are struggling with connectedness. Parents are wounded, so their relationships with their children are disconnected. Things are chaotic, and families don't know what to do.

Parents, it's OK if connectedness doesn't happen every time in every interaction. In fact, it won't. You will make mistakes; you will not be able to give your children what they need all the time. This is good for them if you know how to correct your mistakes. I had a mentor tell me about a client she once had who said her parents were perfect; they did everything right and she had no issues with them. My mentor said, "That is a pity. Your parents' mistakes make you stronger." Be real; don't follow a script; if you make a mistake, talk to your child about it. If you don't, they will see right through you and will smell your inauthenticity a mile away. You must create the reflection you want to see in your child.

Be the reflection you want to see.

My favorite question to ask a parent I'm working with is, "What happens to you when your child_____?" They describe pain from their own childhood in how they were treated when they did what their child is doing. Without fail, every parent has a story of how something didn't go right in their childhood. About how they were treated, their anger met with more anger. Their sadness was dismissed and they were told to stop crying without learning how to self-soothe. Many parents are surprised by their reaction when I ask that question. They think about themselves in relation to their child for the first time. It's a perspective shift. When a parent brings a child to therapy, the child typically is the scapegoat, the one with the diagnosis. The problem. When I ask that question, parents recognize that they have a part in what is happening with their child.

I recall a father I worked with who struggled to discipline his boys when their behavior was out of control. He was at a loss and found himself walking away from situations where he needed to be present. Disappearing. I commended him on walking away because, absent any real ways to manage himself, when he described his temper and how he would have handled those situations, it was a healthier choice for him to disengage. His wife felt alone in parenting their children because his only answer was to disappear, go somewhere else, sometimes physically and always emotionally. He did not know why he was reacting this way and felt powerless to stop it. I asked him, "How were you treated when you needed discipline?" He paused. I could tell he hadn't thought about it before. He then became emotional, started crying, and said, "Not very well." He then described verbal and physical abuse at the hands of his father.

His boys were the ones in therapy at the time. Early on I asked to work with the parents. I saw that the problem wasn't the boys, and I knew I could work with them for years and never get anywhere. They were being typical kids. They were simply reacting to their father's disappearance.

The more he ignored their behavior, the more they wanted to get his attention. They felt the disconnection and were searching for a connection with him. Sometimes the boys were in the room for these conversations. They heard their father break down when I asked about his childhood. I could see the relief in their eyes to know they weren't the "problem." It was their father's issue to work out so he could be more present.

The family was able to heal from that point on. It didn't take very long for their roles to change. The mother felt she had a partner; the father felt he could have control over himself and how he reacted to his children. Most importantly, the children felt that they were allowed to be kids, make mistakes, have bad behavior, and learn from it. The father was able to discipline appropriately with love and support, not with anger and resentment.

Parents must take responsibility for themselves, their feelings, and their behaviors in relation to their children. Only then can children begin to take responsibility for themselves. Remember, parents are the container; your children are shaped inside of you. You must be grounded and together, so your children can learn how to grow themselves. So many parents today are disconnected from themselves, numbing with alcohol, marijuana, social media, and even streaming TV. Disconnected from their lives because things are hard and stressful. Children are being given tacit permission to do the same. The whole family is ill from an overabundance of digital technology, junk food, and media. Media that terrifies them every day to allow their child independence. Something they so desperately need and don't have. Their childhoods being stolen from them.

Be reflective of the age of your child when you struggle in your parenting.

Being a mother felt so natural to me. My whole life I was surrounded by younger children. Later, when I became a mother myself, my cousin said, "You were always meant to be a mother; you're a natural." I knew exactly what she meant. She remembered how I took care of my brother, but motherhood felt hard. It was not like I had imagined it. Like many mothers I was bewildered by the way it felt. I didn't feel like a natural, and I wondered if I was cut out for it.

It got particularly hard when my oldest turned nine. I found myself expecting some independence and responsibility from him. Getting up and getting ready for school on his own, cleaning up after himself, and doing his homework. Those things weren't happening. They weren't happening because I hadn't taught him independence well enough in his younger years. He was an only child until the age of five. I did a lot of developmental tasks for him. I didn't allow him to work through his frustration enough to get to the other side of it and gain autonomy.

It's no wonder I took on caretaking of my brother at this age without being asked. I was his self-appointed second mother. Developmentally, at almost nine, I craved the ability to do things on my own. I received so much good attention for it that it encouraged me to continue.

In a family with five children, that was a way that I could stand out, rather than get lost in the sea of my siblings' personalities. This was all subconscious at the time. I've only come to realize it in adulthood through my experience with motherhood.

My expectation of my son at nine was somewhat unreasonable. What I should have said was, "I learned independence earlier than you in my childhood, and my expectation from you at nine is that you are responsible for yourself. I was not only responsible for myself, but I took care of my younger brother. I was too young to take responsibility for someone else. I don't expect that of you; I only expect you to take care of yourself. It's not your fault that I didn't teach you how to grow. Let's work together on this. What do you need to be OK with doing things on your own? I will help support you, but I won't do it for you." If I had said that, he would have gained confidence in himself and been more willing not only to care for himself but to help with family chores and be of service to the family.

What I didn't know then that I know now is that parenthood is *supposed* to be hard. If it's hard, that's how you know you're doing it right. It's hard because your childhood underdevelopment will manifest itself in the way you feel about your child. Parenthood is a series of projections of the way you feel about yourself. What are you actually trying to say when you use "when I was your age" statements? You are likely trying to say you love your child and you want them to be better off than you. You want them to know how hard you work at making their childhood better than yours.

We can't run away from ourselves. The disconnect we feel in ourselves disconnects us from our children. It disconnects us from our instincts. It allows us to follow advice from people who don't know our children as well as we do. Our generation of parents is overworked, overburdened, burned-out, overcompensating for a childhood we didn't have, and overall apathetic. This is creating families that are not well. Not whole. Parents opting to be their children's friends, giving them what they want, making them happy and comfortable out of a desire to avoid their own discomfort.

I have heard parents say, "Tell me what to do, I just want to know what to do." Word for word, like a script. There is no script, there is no template. I will give you all the information I know, everything I've learned from seeing children for over twenty years in therapy, but you must do the hard work, every day!

We must allow ourselves to be uncomfortable in our own pain, so we can hold the space for our children to be uncomfortable in their pain. We can take back our power and follow our instincts by reflecting on ourselves, our childhood wounds, what keeps us stuck in not parenting holistically. We must see our children for who they are, not how they reflect in us.

I know it's hard.

I struggle with it every day.

I make mistakes.

You will too.

There is no easy way out.

Parenting is hard, and the only out is through.

KEY TAKEAWAYS

- ▸ Your children are a mirror reflecting your childhood wounds.
- ▸ Work through the holes in your development.
- ▸ If you're struggling to parent a certain age, it's likely because you had unresolved developmental issues at that same age.
- ▸ Working through your discomfort and resolving your past will lead to a deeper connection with your children.

CHAPTER 2

THE FOUR PARTS OF CHILD DEVELOPMENT

*We worry about what a child will
become tomorrow, yet we forget
that he is someone today.*[5]
—STACIA TAUSCHER

HAVE YOU EVER WONDERED WHY KIDS TEND TO START preschool when they are three? Or why at five they go to kindergarten, a twelve-year-old enters middle school, a fourteen-year-old goes to high school, at sixteen they drive, and at twenty-one they are given permission to drink alcohol? There are developmental reasons for all of this. The ages at which children are given more independence and separation are appropriate because of child development.

So many parents seek therapy when it isn't needed. By understanding the basis for child development, parents can help their kids through most developmental challenges without the need for diagnosis and professional treatment. Allow them their feelings, even the negative ones, and don't shy away from letting them be uncomfortable in their pain. The only way *out* is *through*, and pain cannot be avoided. There is a lot of strength in realizing and accepting that.

I've learned over the years that a child's mental health cannot be looked at myopically. It's not just the brain, it's not just psychology. We humans are not divided up into parts. We are a whole. The child is a whole; a physical, emotional, spiritual, and energetic being. In my quest to understand this more deeply I have learned how children physically develop, because it's in the physical development that a child's brain grows, and when a child's brain grows the way it needs to then they can develop emotionally and later connect to themselves. I have developed a four-part framework to explain how children develop holistically. In this chapter you will learn about movement.

On a primitive level, children's bodies aren't developing today, physically and cognitively. Research shows that the gray matter in their brains isn't developing because of the use of technology early in life. Gray matter is in the brain and spinal cord, which are in the central nervous system and play a key role in mental functions, memory, emotions, and movement. It is responsible for central nervous system processing. A study done at Cincinnati Children's Hospital Medical Center in 2022 of kids ages three to five suggests that digital media is responsible for hindering the development of brain areas that control visual processing, empathy, attention, complex memory, and early reading skills.[6]

The following diagram describes my method to explain child development in all its parts. It's in the shape of a wheel because each part of development leads to the next. It's important that children go through this wheel as naturally as possible, without the distractions of digital technology to which most of today's children are exposed. In addition to technology's tenacles preventing developmental growth, many parents, in their efforts to keep their children comfortable, are doing the tasks of development for their children. I wish for parents to understand what children need and when they need it; it's imperative to their growth and maturity.

Primitive reflexes and movement

Primitive reflexes and movement develop first; this leads to cognitive or brain development, which then allows for social emotional development and, finally, a connection to self. A connection to self occurs from childhood individuation. Many children today are not experiencing natural child developmental processes and are searching for external stimuli to fill the void of a childhood stolen from them. They are displaying mental and physical health symptoms not rooted in anything on the surface. Each of these stages of development needs to be complete as a foundation for

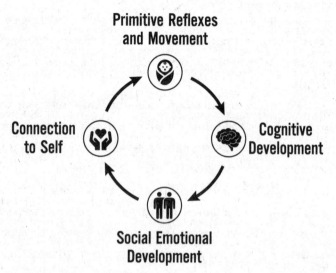

Source: Nicole Runyon

children to grow and mature. Children must move through development without too much interruption. If they get most of what they need they will be independent, healthy adults. If their development is disrupted too frequently, they will have a multitude of issues that can look like mental illness. I would like to give you a deeper look into the root causes so you can help your child either prevent issues from occurring or change the landscape for them if they are already encountering mental health problems.

> **Movement scaffolds the brain for growth.**
> —*Dr. BG Mancini,*
> *The Family Nervous System*

Birth to three years

Innately, we are born with primitive reflexes that allow us to survive. Primitive reflexes are reactions that originate in the central nervous system. These reflexes are necessary for the body to develop and should be integrated by the end of infancy, though some do not fully integrate until three and a half years as we enter childhood. Primitive reflexes should grow into a mature, more voluntary movement as the child grows. Babies start out with reflexes for survival. For example, when touched on the sides of their mouth, babies begin "rooting" to find food. You will see them turn their heads in the direction of the touch to indicate to their caregiver that they are hungry. When a baby is more developed in their movement to find food, they no longer need the rooting reflex, and it should become integrated. Integrated means the reflex fades into the nervous system but doesn't go away. When babies are between three and four months old, their sensory motor skills develop enough not to need to root as a form of survival. If they are developing within the normal range, they are moving with tummy time and rolling over. Their bodies can find food in other ways.

In the first year of life babies need their primitive reflexes. By three and a half they are expected to have crawled and walked, and are starting to run, jump, climb, and skip. Many children today are retaining their reflexes. This means the reflexes don't integrate or fade into the nervous system. The following chart depicts some physical, cognitive, and mental health consequences of retained reflexes.

Reflex	Purpose	Age Appears	Age Integrates	Signs of Retention
Moro Reflex	Fight or flight reaction, sympathetic nervous system response	Birth	2–4 months	Hypersensitivity to one or more sensory systems, vestibular deficits (motion sickness, poor coordination and balance), oculomotor or visual-perceptual problems, poor pupillary reaction to light, hypersensitivity to auditory input, allergies and lowered immunity, adverse drug reactions, poor stamina, poor adaptability, reactive hypoglycemia
Rooting Reflex	Autonomic response to locate food and breast	Birth	3–4 months	Anterior tongue tie; thumb-sucking; oral hypersensitivity; poor eating, speech, and articulation problems; swallowing and chewing deficits
Palmar Grasp Reflex	Autonomic flexion of the fingers to grab when the palm is stimulated	Birth	3–6 months	Poor manual dexterity, deficits with pencil grip, poor visual coordination, poor posture during handwriting, poor writing skills, correlated speech and hand movements, dysfunction of the tactile and proprioceptive sensory systems
Asymmetric Tonic Neck Reflex (ATNR)	Assists with movement through the birth canal at delivery and is important for cross pattern movements	Birth	6 months	Decreased hand-eye coordination, poor handwriting, uncoordinated gait, poor balance, poor visual motor skills and tracking, problems with math and reading, difficulty crossing midline
Spinal Galant Reflex	Important during the birthing process and helps to facilitate movement of the hips during descending the birthing canal	Birth	3–9 months	Postural issues such as scoliosis, misaligned or rotated pelvis, and pain in lower back, bedwetting after potty training, hyperactivity, attention and concentration issues, decreased endurance, chronic digestive issues, decreased lower body coordination, pain and tension in legs
Tonic Labyrinthine Reflex (TNR)	Foundational for postural stability of large muscle groups	In utero	3½ years	Decreased balance, poor spatial awareness, toe walking, hypermobility of joints, weak muscles, poor posture, motion sickness, poor ability to climb, atypical head position (forward or to side)
Landau Reflex	Necessary for postural development	4–5 months	1 year	Poor posture and muscle tone, somersaults are challenging, poor coordination for activities that require upper body and lower body to move together, delayed motor development
Symmetric Tonic Neck Reflex (STNR)	Foundational for crawling	6–9 months	9–11 months	Poor posture in standing, poor seated posture, apelike walk, low muscle tone, W sitting position is common, sloppy/messy eater, poor hand-eye coordination

Original chart source from Samantha Heidenreich's "Understanding Primitive Reflexes." [7]

Infancy (birth to age 1)

Movement is being restricted with today's children at each stage of development because of technology, manipulative marketing, and poor parenting advice. This lack of movement starts in infancy. There are numerous ways parents are seduced into buying contraptions claiming safety, good sleep, and healthy development for their babies and toddlers. There are smart bassinets, smart chairs, walkers, jumpers, and swings—the options are almost endless. With my first child, I had all the contraptions that I had growing up, thinking they were benign. The swing, the walker, the jumper. My son, my oldest, had good intuition and enough sense to know he needed to move. He hated being put in anything that wasn't my arms, the floor, or a set of stairs. He crawled, climbed, jumped, ran, made messes, and got dirty. I resigned myself to knowing I was not going to get anything done until he was able to be mobile without my supervision. I knew the smart devices were not a good idea, but I fell for the marketing on all the others. By the time my second child came around I had learned that free movement was the best way for a baby to develop. She was able to move and explore just like her brother.

These devices exist as young as infant age. Many young parents are seduced by the marketing of a product that boasts a sound night's sleep and mental clarity for the tired parent. One smart sleeper bassinet claims the following in its advertisement…

- "**Adds 1–2 hours of sleep per night** with constant calming womb rhythms."
- "**Secure swaddling** prevents rolling to an unsafe position during sleep."
- "Soothes with motion + sound, **often calming crying in under a minute.**"
- "**Automatically responds to baby's needs** when it detects fussing or crying."
- "Ready 24/7, **teaches baby to self-soothe** with little need to cry-it-out."
- "Finally, research in the journal *PLOS ONE* concluded that swaddling, sound, and movement work equally well for soothing babies, whether it comes from the smart sleeper bassinet or a loving adult…making the smart sleeper bassinet a much-needed helper for parents whose 'village' is too far away to offer middle-of-the-night soothing that allows weary parents to rest."[8]

Babies are strapped in and unable to move their arms and legs, their innate and necessary reflexes to survive. This can cause distress and anxiety later in life because it completely takes away all control over their bodies that they have. Control of their reflexes, their survival mechanism. We wonder why we have an anxiety epidemic. It starts here. With this mentality.

In this advertisement each of the bullet points is worse than the one before. Take the first: "constant calming womb rhythms." That should be a parent's arms, soothing sounds from their voice and the comfort of real human connection. A mother's body and voice are the only things that mimic the womb, not a machine. This is what makes the nervous system feel safe and is a necessary part of sensory development.

The smart sleeper bassinet is not a replacement for a loving adult, as this ad claims. The next one, "secure swaddling," is also concerning. If a baby can roll over from his back to his belly, he can certainly roll from his belly to his back. Babies aren't going to suffocate themselves once they can roll over. If you put them on their back to sleep, they will stay there until they are ready to move more; then they will put themselves where they need to be.

Then, "soothes with motion and sound." The caregiver soothes. It's integral to attachment and bonding.

"Automatically responds to baby's needs." Again, the caregiver, a real human being, responds to baby's needs.

Lastly, "self-soothing." This shouldn't occur until eighteen months. From birth to eighteen months, babies are in the attachment phase of development. This is when a caregiver must respond to their needs. It's what builds trust and sets the stage for how the baby trusts others in future relationships. Self-soothing comes later. A machine should never replace that process.

If the smart sleeper bassinet was the only smart device that detached babies from their caregivers, it might not be permanently damaging. Harlow's study with rhesus monkeys depicts a scenario where monkeys are separated at birth from their mothers and given access to two different surrogate mothers, one made from wire and the other covered in soft terry cloth. The wire "mothers" had food, and the terry cloth mothers did not. The study concluded that the monkeys preferred the terry cloth mothers over the wire mothers. They ate from the wire mothers and sought comfort from the terry cloth mothers. They spent more time with the terry cloth mothers overall. Moreover, the researchers conducted a second experiment where they separated the monkeys into two groups, leaving one group with the wire mothers and the other feeding from the wire mother but mostly with the terry cloth mother. Both groups were fed well and grew physically the same; however, the monkeys that had access to the food and no comfort were timid, didn't know how to act with other monkeys, were easily bullied, wouldn't stand up for themselves, and had difficulty mating. The females were inadequate mothers. Here's the part that relates to the smart sleeper bassinet: The study showed "these behaviors were observed only in the monkeys who were left with the surrogate mothers for more than 90 days. For those left less than 90 days, the effects could be reversed if placed in a normal environment where they could form attachments."[9]

The smart sleeper bassinet is only the beginning of a childhood on technology. If it were just that it would be damaging, but the damage could be reversed. A childhood of developmental milestones being reached with an attached caregiver is what a child needs. That is not what is happening. Today's children called the iGeneration

(Internet generation) and today's teenagers dubbed "screen-agers" are being raised on technology from the moment they leave the womb. They are experiencing a childhood that is changing their development. Their brains are liter-ally not developing gray matter. They are void of movement starting in infancy. They are put in a smart sleeper bassinet at birth, given a tablet as early as ten months, given head-sets to go with their tablets at two, shut off from all access to the sensory stimuli in their surroundings, and deprived of all their senses for long periods. We wonder why so many kids are experiencing sensory processing issues. They are then provided a laptop at five for school and given a smart device as early as eight. What are we doing? Restricted movement causes several problems for chil-dren. Problems that aren't being treated correctly because our mainstream healthcare system doesn't address it. We must stop looking at the brain and the brain's psychology as a separate part.

Lack of movement in infancy and childhood was a problem before the lockdown of 2020 and reached a tipping point when parents had to work from home during the lockdowns. With parents in front of screens all day, babies' movements were restricted, many of them not meeting developmental milestones during a critical period. Many young children were being put in front of a screen so parents could work. There were so many babies who weren't crawling at the appropriate age that the Centers for Disease Control and Prevention (CDC) changed its criteria and took crawling completely off the list of milestones. I and my colleagues think this is absurd. Crawling is very important for integrating the primitive reflex of crossing the midline of the body. Crossing the midline means physically moving the opposite arm with the opposite leg. You can also cross the left arm and leg over to the right side of the body and vice versa, with the right arm and leg crossing the left side of the body. This physicality allows both sides of the brain to work together to process information. The ramifications of taking crawling off the developmental milestones are endless. Crawling is so important and necessary for a healthy development.

This is important information for parents to understand because this is happening on a physical level. Many children exhibit learning problems, attention and focus issues, and anxiety and nervous system regulation issues, which can all look psychological and affect neurology. These symptoms are not always rooted in a psychological issue though they are often treated in the mental health system to no avail. I have been seeing a growing number of kids with this issue who weren't responding to treatment. Kids are pathologized, labeled, psychologically tested, and given a cocktail of psychotropic pharmaceuticals. Parents need to know so they can receive the right kind of help because in cases where children are experiencing these symptoms from reflex retention, lack of sensory motor integration, and gut inflammation from lack of nutrition, psychotherapy not only doesn't work, it can also make things worse. Before I understood this, I spun my wheels in therapy with cases that had no psychosocial root. The child often felt shame and was pathologized for something they didn't know how to fix. Nor did I. Parents grew frustrated and I became burned out and had feelings of inadequacy because I didn't know how to help. I ruled out trauma histories before I stated to dig deeper into what might be going on.

My physical therapy, occupational therapy, and speech therapy colleagues report issues in their patients independent of anything medical. More and more children are behind on all physical milestones and speech milestones. Professional providers have similar stories to mine. They have been practicing for years and have seen an uptick in these issues since screens became more prevalent in children's lives. The following is a quote from a colleague of mine, Donna Dotson, who gave me permission to share this to educate parents on the effects of screens on physical development.

> I have been a physical therapist at Children's Hospital of Michigan for twenty-nine years. I have been witnessing a disturbing trend in the children I see at work. In the past, the children we saw with challenges had a medical diagnosis to explain the cause. In more recent years we are seeing more and more children with a variety of challenges who have no diagnosis. I began referring to them as "broken children" because it appeared that they were born "normal" but then something went wrong. In interviewing families, the common theme is excessive screen time. This trend has gotten worse year by

year, with the pandemic pushing everyone over the brink. "Broken children" now make up roughly half my caseload. These are children with gross motor, fine motor, and speech delays, attention and focus issues, behavioral problems, vision problems, and toe walking, with no medical cause.

During this critical period, parents should allow their babies and toddlers to move as much as possible. Movement can be inconvenient for parents. It requires you to put your devices down, look up, and engage, but the best safety for your baby and toddler is *you*! A device that entertains, a contraption that holds them down, will never replace you. Parents, you are enough for them. You are everything they need.

Another key role for parents: Help your children connect to nature. Get them playing outside as much as possible. Babies can be held or walked in a stroller. Babies who are crawling can be put down in grassy areas. You can try a blanket, but my kids never stayed on the blanket; they wanted to roam! Nature is a necessary part of their development during this time, as nature enhances their physical development and allows their central nervous system to develop sensory processing.

Ages 3-7

I learned the following information from Charlotte Davies, who founded Fit-2-Learn. I discovered her work when I was researching a case I was stuck on. Traditional therapies weren't working for this child. My mind was blown when I learned about sensory motor integration. Her treatment entails primitive reflex exercises, visual processing exercises, and sound therapy for auditory processing issues.

When reflexes don't integrate, children don't process sensory information as they should. Their eyes don't work together to process visual information to the brain as fast as they need to, causing visual-processing disorders. Their ears don't work together to process auditory information to the brain, and their bodies have trouble crossing the midline, so both sides of the brain don't work together to fire information quickly. The midline is a medical term referring to the center plane in the body that divides it into halves, the right side and the left side. Crawling is the first movement a baby makes to develop crossing the midline. When children don't have proper sensory motor integration, slow sensory processing ensues, and this wreaks havoc on a child, as developmentally they are sensory beings until the age of seven. From the ages of two to seven, children develop their sensory processing through physical play.

Kids with this issue don't respond to traditional therapy because they have trouble regulating. They feel overwhelmed in their bodies. Traditional therapy would have kids learn how to express and communicate their feelings appropriately before a meltdown. Humans learn certain vocabulary for feelings over time, but many kids don't have the words to describe how they feel. Once they can describe it, then they can learn how to recognize those feelings inside of themselves and learn coping skills for when they are feeling unregulated. We talk about what they can do with those feelings, what they can control, and what their part is. This allows them to feel in control of themselves and makes it easier to regulate their feelings. This doesn't work for children who are experiencing integration issues. Their brains can't process that information because their bodies aren't supporting it. Children should be developing and learning language for their feelings during this time. They will be a bit wobbly and struggle with it. It will be uncomfortable.

How do you know if your child is experiencing integration issues or simply having a difficult time expressing and communicating feelings? How do you know if it's a mental health issue or a physical issue? Mental health issues are rooted in trauma. If your family is intact and there is no history of abuse, neglect, or a known trauma, chances are your child's mental health symptoms are a result of some other issue. In a later chapter I will describe actual trauma versus childhood difficulties, as *trauma* is a buzzword and is often misunderstood. Many children with symptoms of ADD/ADHD and even autism are not experiencing mental health issues per se; they are struggling with their bodies not supporting their brain growth. Many children with this issue appear to be oppositional and noncompliant; as a result, they are often misdiagnosed as oppositional defiant disorder and even conduct disorder. These diagnoses indicate that children are unable to have respect or care for their caretakers. But those are trauma reactions and should not be diagnosed for a child with no known trauma who cannot regulate themselves due to physical issues.

Some symptoms to look for are extreme, sudden-onset outbursts of emotion. I have seen these issues materialize in this age range. If they were present before, they become more magnified. Many kids who are mild mannered one minute can explode in the next. They have trouble regulating their feelings, so if they are told "no" to something they want or they are told to do something they don't want to do, they tend to flip a switch and yell, kick, throw things, physically harm their siblings and/or their parents, and use expletives. When they come out of their rage, they often don't remember what happened, as if they were experiencing an out-of-body event.

What I see happening to families with kids who experience this debilitating issue is heartbreaking. Often because of their behavior, their families become resentful of them. They feel one child is controlling the entire family. The entire family is at the mercy of the child struggling with regulating their feelings. Families describe not being able to go anywhere for fear of public meltdowns. They feel trapped. Often siblings in these families develop perfectionist qualities because they don't want to be trouble for their parents, knowing that their parents already have enough trouble. Siblings tend to be anxious and don't express it because the parents are usually overwhelmed. Parents often express guilt for feeling resentful and angry with their child. All efforts to help are thwarted by one bad moment. Parents feel desperate, powerless.

School-age children 5-12

It is estimated that one in four school-going children suffer from developmental delays/deficits, such as difficulty communicating, language problems, impaired motor skills, and emotional deficits, as well as learning disabilities, due to excessive screen time. Why is this happening to so many children of the iGeneration, aka Generation Z (born 1997–2012) and Generation Alpha (born 2012 to the present)? A healthy brain grows with each developmental phase of childhood. Neurological developmental disorders are created when there is a disruption to the development along the way. Early and frequent use of screens disrupts brain growth. Screens affect the way the brain grows structurally and functionally. This should be very concerning to parents, educators, and society as a whole. Children need to develop without being distracted by a screen's blue light, overstimulation, loud noises coming from a screen, and cartoonish music when they are playing a game. Nor do they need to learn their ABCs and 123s on a device. They need human interaction, bonding with their caregivers, running, jumping, playing, exploring, digging, climbing, swimming, exploring nature, to be read to by human voices, sleeping, and healthy eating.

If you have a school-age child, you may have given them a solid foundation of screen limits, proper nutrition, and outdoor play. They then enter school and are placed inside a building for most of the day, cut off from nature and separated from their natural biorhythms. They are also likely exposed to foods lacking in nutrients and to screens. Many school districts have decreased recess time, and children are receiving less outdoor play throughout the day. You may see an otherwise engaged healthy child lose some of their good nature as a result. Here's where I remind you: You know your child better than anyone; you know what they need and when they need it. If you are experiencing this with your child, there are ways to navigate. The answer will be different for every family, but as a rule you can help your child in the following ways:

- Advocate for your child to do schoolwork and/ or homework off digital devices. You can always opt out of computer work for worksheets and paperwork.
- Talk to other parents! A community of parents who are seeing negative effects of limited movement in their children is better than only one of us.
- Homeschool is a great option for parents who can do so. There are co-ops and homeschool groups that meet regularly so kids can socialize and learn from other parents.

Age 12 and beyond

Movement is important at any age. If adolescents don't participate in a physical extracurricular activity, they are not getting enough physical activity. Recess time is not prioritized in most middle schools and high schools. Lunch time is cut down, so children are scarfing their food down, leaving no room to rest and digest, a necessary part of nervous system regulation. Many districts across the country have changed physical education requirements to be an elective, and many kids consider it a "blow off" class. Children are getting little to no movement during their school day. When they come home, they game online, chat with one another online, and remain sedentary the rest of the day.

There was a time in America when everyone, including the government, was on board with children being physically strong and healthy. President John F. Kennedy wanted children to grow up with "vigor and energy." He wanted to make America strong, starting with the children. He instituted a national physical fitness program.[10] He feared a day in the future when American citizens were mostly spectators. I can't imagine he had any idea that his fear would come true. So many children are watching, remaining on the sidelines, not feeling capable.

The following are some of the challenges Kennedy instituted into physical fitness programs in school across the nation.

- Boys age 6: 33 curl-ups
- Boys age 16: 8.7-second shuttle run
- Girls age 8: +4.5 inches v-sit reach
- Girls age 15: 8:08-minute mile run

Awards were offered for meeting the requirements in each category. The challenges were hard. It was something to work toward, and if you accomplished the goal, you received a sense of pride and confidence. My husband remembers his high school gym class this way. When he recalled the exercises, he was amazed at how hard they were, and then sad to see just how few physical challenges today's children receive, as this fitness challenge is long gone in schools.

Big Tech is profiting off our children spending numerous hours a day on its products. The tech industry is profiting off children being sick and weak. Parents, I urge you to think not just about what your kids are exposed to online, but what they are not doing because they are spending so much time on a screen.

They are not moving.

Parents, don't wait for things to change. Protect your children by pushing them out of their comfort zones and into more movement every day. Instill exercise as a way of life.

Lastly, if you feel your child is struggling with retained reflexes due to lack of movement, you can find a practitioner to do an evaluation for retained reflexes, trouble with midline crossing, and visual and/or auditory dysfunction. There are resources online where you can find primitive reflex exercises to foster integration. Also, you can find a practitioner who works with Safe and Sound protocol (SSP) designed by Dr. Stephen Porges. This is a program using sound to help calm the nervous system so it can feel safe to process sensory information and regulate the emotional center. There are also practitioners who do Tomatis sound therapy. This treatment is a series of sound waves developed strategically that is played from a headset into the ears. This strengthens sound processing so that both ears can work together to process auditory information to the brain.

KEY TAKEAWAYS

- ▸ Primitive reflexes and movement are needed early on to help children develop their central nervous system.
- ▸ Restricting movement at any age leads to a decline in physical, mental, and cognitive development, causing several issues for children and families.
- ▸ Children have unique needs at certain ages for movement; these are critical windows of development.
- ▸ Parents need to connect to their instincts and give children ample opportunity to physically move.

CHAPTER 3

FAMILY HEALTH

*What most people don't realize is that
food is not just calories: It's information.
It actually contains messages that
communicate to every cell in the body.*[11]
—Dr. Mark Hyman

A CHILDHOOD SPENT INDOORS ON SCREENS, LACKING movement, isn't healthy. In addition, many children today lack proper nutrition in their diets, the foundation for all of child development. Nutrients feed the brain. Babies need a diet rich in nutrients; it's vital as their brains are growing rapidly in the first six years. Nutrient-rich foods include fruits and vegetables, proteins, and good fats, as well as complex carbs such as sweet potatoes and beans. Childhood obesity is at an all-time high. "Approximately 1 in 5 US children and adolescents have obesity."[12] The body positivity movement will have you think this is OK. The reality is that being overweight is unhealthy at any age, especially in childhood. Obesity increases risk for type 2 diabetes, heart disease, and cancer. This generation of children is expected to be the first not to outlive their parents!

Early on, a child's first foods are marketed as kid food and placed in fun, colorful packaging that makes parents think they are distinct from adult food. Baby food companies manufacture snacks made with simple carbohydrates such as puffs, teething wafers, fruit and vegetable pouches, yogurt bites, and sugary drinks, all made with ingredients such as processed wheat fortified with synthetic vitamins, sugar, inflammatory seed oils, and artificial flavors and colors. The seductive packaging claims "organic, real fruit juice and whole grain."

But these packaged foods are not rich in nutrients. The manufacturers have taken ingredients that exist in nature, which alone are healthy, and made them into a highly addictive snack, training babies, toddlers, and children to develop a palate that prefers added sugar. Real fruit does not taste as sweet as a package of fruit snacks. Remember when the tobacco companies told people smoking was good for them? They said it aided in weight loss and would help keep you calm. Their sophisticated advertising has now been transferred to the soft drink and food companies. They bought food companies and now use the same strategies to market to children. For example, a popular sugary drink linked to childhood obesity was manufactured by a big tobacco company until the mid-2000s. While those companies have split their food businesses from tobacco business, the same marketing techniques are embedded in the company.[13]

Many of today's children are picky eaters because they are fed a diet of ultra-processed, sugary foods early on. I fed my kids homemade baby food purée, and when they could chew, I fed them what we ate, real food. People were amazed at how they ate whatever was put in front of them, my oldest even preferring spicy food as young as one. Both became picky eaters almost immediately when they attended preschool because they were exposed to packaged foods at school. This made their palates prefer processed foods over real whole foods.

Big Food profits off busy, overwhelmed parents who want to feed their children healthy food but don't make the time to prepare it. They have the solution: convenience. For example, pre-packaged containers of lunch meat, cheese, and crackers and packages of premade peanut butter-and-jelly sandwiches with the crusts cut off all promise parents an easy way to feed their children. These products all have a long list of ingredients, some of which are hard to pronounce. Their clever marketing, such as placing kids' movie characters on the packaging and promises of protein servings and guaranteed freshness, make it easy for parents to give their children what they want to avoid the food battle. The companies make packaged food addictive to keep tired, busy parents coming back to please their children. Just to make parents' lives a little bit easier.

Kids' meals are often void of nutrition. Think of the color of a typical kid food plate: chicken nuggets, French fries, buttered noodles, and bread. There is a reason the standard American diet is called "SAD." A plate full of brown and yellow is not exciting or beautiful; rather, it's sad. Alternatively, think of a plate with delicata squash, green beans cooked in a tasty tomato sauce, and white fish with capers and olives. Yellow, green, red, white all on one plate. Or, if your family is vegetarian, replace the fish with chickpeas and beans in the tomato sauce dish. That's beautiful. I always found the idea of feeding kids a brown diet insulting to them. They absolutely *can* learn to love a healthy plate of food. Food and eating are tough, of course, because you don't want your child to starve if they refuse to eat anything other than brown food.

When we differentiate adult food from kid food, we really do the children a disservice. While we think we are making them happy in the short term, it leads to long-term health issues. "Kid food" is known to cause inflammation in the body. This leads to leaky gut and triggers the gut/brain connection, a term many of you have heard but likely don't know the science behind. My colleague BG Mancini has some great information on this subject. Her company, the Brain Gut Institute, specializes in pediatric mental health. She explains the science behind how leaky gut affects the brain. Gut inflammation leads to brain inflammation. With brain inflammation, mental health symptoms ensue. This is because gut inflammation triggers the autonomic nervous system to go into fight-or-flight mode. If a child's body is constantly inflamed, they will constantly be in fight-or-flight mode and exhibit symptoms of mental illness, such as anxiety. I don't diagnose mental health symptoms in children who have been tested and have a known gut issue. I also don't diagnose mental health issues in kids who lack movement because of too much screen time or unhealthy lifestyle choices. I look at root causes and address them at their core.

What can you do?

Ideally, feed your child whole, nutritious foods at all ages starting with their first foods. Foods rich in helping the body produce a healthy microbiome such as probiotic-rich foods, vegetables, and good fats such as avocados, nuts, and seeds. However, if you started out with processed foods and they are picky eaters, I suggest trying healthy foods more often while saying no to processed sugary foods. Saying no to unhealthy food will not cause an eating disorder. It is setting a limit, it's a boundary, it's telling your child you care about their health, and you will not allow them to eat junk food because it's poison.

Parents can curb picky eating by having kids try different foods and flavors on a regular basis. It's been said that you must try something twelve times, twelve different ways, before your palate becomes used to it and you enjoy eating it. I know that might seem overwhelming. Be consistent with having them try different foods and before you know it, it will open them up to try more. If you feed them sugary, processed foods regularly, they will never learn to like nutritious foods. One major issue I see is that anywhere there are kids, there is junk food. As a society we must be better at nourishing children, so they grow to be strong and healthy. Kids don't need a sugary, processed snack after a sports practice or game, during the school day as a reward for listening or answering a question correctly, after getting a haircut, or simply for existing and breathing!

I counseled a family in my practice who struggled with mealtime. The parents, both working, were chronically stressed and gave in to their children's picky eating. This caused them to feel they had to make two meals to keep their children happy. The parents were well intentioned and feared their children would be malnourished if they didn't do things this way. I suggested that the children accompany the parents to the grocery store with one rule: They had to pick out one healthy ingredient they liked and help their parents make a meal out of it. They could look up recipes, find things they like in the recipe, and build a meal out of it. Then they had to help their parents cook the meal and at least try it. A healthy ingredient was defined as a fruit, vegetable, or protein. Basically, the outer perimeter of the grocery store. Nothing in the aisles, as that is where the packaged food lives. The parents reported it went swimmingly well, and the children chose carrots. They made a nutritious meal together incorporating the carrots!

Children are sensitive to external toxins because their brains are still developing. Junk food particularly affects their behavior. This causes me to recall the worst session I ever had. This session was with a nine-year-old client who entered my office while eating a sugary snack packed with artificial flavors and colors. Almost immediately she was unable to sit still, laughed uncontrollably, and could not pull herself together enough to have a session. I ended up calling her parent in to take her home, rendering the session ineffective. If you watch your children after they've eaten processed foods, you *will* see a change in them, whether behavioral or emotional. They will likely come down from the blood sugar spike, be lethargic, and even possibly depressed. So many ADD/ADHD diagnoses are because of reactions to food. Toxic food crosses the blood-brain barrier and affects attention and focus in children. If your children are eating a breakfast void of nutrition, such as cereal or toaster pastries, they are likely not going to be able to sit still and pay attention in school.

One easy change you can make to a diet high in simple carbohydrates and sugar is to add protein, especially if your child is having trouble sleeping. Many parents report their children have trouble getting up in the morning and going to sleep at night. They are irritable upon waking and have low frustration tolerance at bedtime. Mornings and nights are hard, and meltdowns often happen before school and before bed. When a parent reports behavior problems, meltdowns, conflict, screaming, and even violent behavior, my first question is, "How are they sleeping?" Sleep is foundational. If a child is tired, they will have low frustration tolerance and struggle with dysregulation. The number one symptom children and parents report to me is being tired. A huge cause of this is diet. Many children are experiencing blood sugar imbalances in the night. If you go to bed after having eaten an overabundance of sugar and carbs all day, at dinner, or even just before bed, as many kids do, you will have trouble falling asleep. Once you fall asleep it is difficult to stay asleep due to blood sugar crashes. The crash wakes you up and tells your body it's time to eat. Protein will help slow the absorption of blood sugar. Protein in the morning can curb difficulty waking, and protein at night can help a child fall asleep and stay asleep through the night restfully.

I advocate for families to incorporate good nutrition, but I want to address that not all families have healthy food available to them. Healthy food is not accessible to children growing up in poverty. Corn, soybeans, wheat, rice, and sugar are all subsidized by the government.[14] These foods are genetically engineered (GMO) to increase crop yields and sprayed with poisonous pesticides to prevent loss caused by pests consuming the produce. This is the basis for the ultra-processed foods that are peddled to parents as kid food. Corn is often turned into high fructose corn syrup, a substance known to cause blood sugar spikes. Once processed, soybeans become phytoestrogens, disrupting hormones in children. The way wheat is processed takes the protein out and makes it hard to digest, the reason for so many wheat sensitivities and allergies.

These products are cheap and shelf-stable, both necessary for parents living in low-income areas where grocery stores are sparse. What if the government subsidized sweet potatoes, broccoli, kale, and chia seeds? These foods would be available to families who otherwise can't afford them. Therefore, I encourage parents to take control of what we can, because waiting for government to take care of our children is harming us all. Big Food and the government are colluding. Calley Means, a former food and pharmaceutical consultant, along with his sister Casey Means, a medical doctor, are on a mission to educate us about the food industry. They are blowing the whistle and exposing "how big pharma co-opted government agencies and the food industry to poison America and keep us sick."[15] In addition to subsidizing crops used to make processed foods, Big Food funds research studies that tell us ultra-processed foods are not bad for our health. Calley Means talks about food and beverage companies funding major research at universities such as Harvard and Stanford. He reports food companies fund nutrition research in the US eleven times more than the National Institutes of Health (NIH) does. He says that researchers are paid bribes to create bias in favor of Big Food.[16] The confusion around food and what is and isn't good for us is intentional. The more confused we are, the more we surrender and give kids what they want. It's exhausting for parents trying to figure out what is right with this information overload.

Parents, here's where your instincts come in. If you see your child's behavior, school or sports performance, mental health, or sleep affected by what they are eating and the lack of nutrition, connect to that. Don't let anyone tell you that children are resilient and can eat these foods. Don't let anyone tell you that your child has an illness that can only be treated by pharmaceuticals. Food is medicine. You know your children better than any doctor, therapist, or double-blind placebo-controlled study!

"Unfortunately, we're living in an environment where many children's brains are not optimizing for these windows of opportunistic development,"[17] writes Delia McCabe, PhD, a former psychologist turned neuroscientist. She continues,

> Childhood should contain lots of unsupervised outdoor play, lots of interaction with peers, lots of communication with family, and lots of physical movement generally and enough sleep. Add to this the high intake of ultra-processed foods among children today, with 67 percent of calories consumed by children coming from such foods, and we can see clearly that optimal brain development is further disadvantaged.
>
> A process called "synaptic pruning" starts occurring after about the age of ten wherein the brain starts "pruning" neuronal connections that have not been used. If these critical windows of development do not proceed smoothly, due to a lack of environmental stimulation and a deficiency in the right nutrients, the child's brain complexity is compromised, and brain development is unable

to unfold smoothly to set the stage for future intelligence.[18]

Teach children the 80/20 rule: 80 percent of the time they should eat healthy, and 20 percent of the time they can have junk food. In full transparency, children should rarely or never have ultra-processed foods—those that contain chemical additives. These chemicals cross the blood-brain barrier, which isn't fully developed in children, so they are more sensitive to synthetic substances. I am, however, a parent and know that these foods are literally *everywhere*! Even when you don't buy them or eat them, unless you live under a rock you can't avoid them altogether. Therefore, I suggest the 80/20 rule or perhaps the 90/10 rule. Whatever works for your family. As your children grow, you will have less control over what they eat. As they are in the world without you more, ideally you want them to make good choices around food and their nutrition. This is easier if you started when they were young, but not impossible. I always talked with my kids about food, mainly because my oldest had food allergies early on. Both of my kids on separate occasions heard me talking about bleached flour and asked, "You mean the flour is bleached?" Each was so grossed out that they avoided it at first, but not for long. These foods are extremely addictive, and kids have trouble setting limits for themselves. I suggest talking to them about health and modeling good health for them. Helping them to make good choices when they grow up. This includes a nutrient-rich diet, regular exercise, and proper sleep.

I know this is asking a lot. My husband I manage three meals a day every day for our two children. We have prioritized healthy food in our family because it is important to us. I assure you I know what it's like to live the hustle and bustle American family life. Our superpower is the connection we have to our children. They trust us. We give them the information about food, and they make decisions for themselves when they are out in the world. We control what is in our home—whole nutritious foods—and outside of the home, armed with the knowledge we've given them, we must trust them to have self-control. Sometimes they do, sometimes they don't. When they don't, they notice the consequences are illness, lack of attention and focus, as well as low frustration tolerance and disrupted sleep.

Co-regulation

The last thing I want is for the information about food and nutrition to cause stress and anxiety. If you feel that you don't know how to make a change, start with yourself. Parents' abilities to regulate ourselves and our feelings transfer to our children. If we are under duress or stress, they will pick up on it. If they are under stress, we must hold the space for them by allowing them their feelings and being the container by being calm so they can calm. This creates connection between parents and children and allows for the family to be healthy together. It is a very tall order and difficult to maintain. I admit this is the hardest part of parenting for me, and I struggle with keeping my stress under control.

We recently moved. It wasn't a very big move, only about three miles. Not much changed in our day-to-day life, so all in all it was a relatively easy move. Compared to an out-of-state relocation several years ago, this was a breeze.

Nonetheless, I found myself having trouble regulating my nervous system. My body was inflamed, I wasn't sleeping, and my hands stopped working at one point. While unpacking a box in the kitchen I dropped a large glass canister of rice and it shattered, sending glass and rice everywhere! Compounded stress and months of not sleeping. We lived in our house for eleven years before this move, and for my youngest it was the only house she'd ever known.

She was excited to move and didn't seem sad about leaving the house she lived in her whole life. I asked her several times if she needed to say goodbye in a special way to help the transition. She said she was good and happy to have a new house.

I thought that was odd and I shared this with a friend. She offered, "She's a well-adjusted kid." That made sense. We moved on a Friday and by that Sunday my well-adjusted nine-year-old, who has a meltdown maybe once a year, melted down three times before 9 a.m. Hmm? At first I thought, *Well, it's an adjustment, of course she's out of sorts.*

Then I thought about how I was so sensitive to her adjustment issues that I stopped us all from unpacking and cleaning on Saturday night to have a family dinner and game night, allowing her to feel the family connection. During dinner she said, "Mom, I feel so content." I had done everything right; why was she melting? Then it hit me! *I* was dysregulated! My stress was over the top, and she was picking up on that.

How did I not recognize that sooner? This is what I speak about, coach parents about, and am an overall expert on. Parents are conductors for our children, we pass down the energy to them. When I was doing therapy with children, I often diagnosed adjustment disorder. Adjustment disorder with anxiety and depressed mood, with mixed disturbance of emotions and conduct. This diagnosis indicates a pathological reaction to a life event or circumstance—a parental divorce, grief and loss of a pet or loved one, a move. I no longer pathologize a normal reaction to something that's hard. Pain is a part of life, a part of transitioning.

Even if it's a good transition it will come with growing pains. It's not disordered. Regarding our family move, I could have gone on under extreme stress for longer, but my daughter made me stop and look at myself. Her behavior was telling me something. She was responding to me. I went back to taking care of myself. I take care of myself for her.

My story is what's happening to today's families every day. The autonomic nervous system is responsible for our survival mechanisms with the fight, flight, freeze, or fawn response (sympathetic nervous system). The other function of the nervous system is the vagus nerve, which is responsible for rest and digestion (parasympathetic). If you must survive something you may stay and fight, which is sometimes appropriate if you are fighting something your own size. If you can run to escape a dangerous situation, then your sympathetic nervous system will take "flight." If you have a trauma history, you may freeze and do nothing, like the deer in the headlights. And if you are trained to be agreeable and helpless as a form of emotional survival, you will "fawn."

When a family dynamic is dysfunctional, it causes the family members to react in fight, flight, freeze, or fawn. Families today are struggling. Overscheduled and undernourished, most of us are walking around carrying stress. This trickles down to our children and can cause inflammation in the body. This inflammation over time damages the nervous system, leaving us struggling with our day-to-day emotions. This feels like chaos, and the outward expression of that is anxiety. In addition to anxiety, an overstimulated, dysregulated nervous system causes mental health issues such as ADD/ADHD, OCD, oppositional defiant disorder, tics, anger spells, and depression.

I had an adolescent client whom we will call Iris. I saw her for two sessions. After we talked, I suggested that her parents participate in parent coaching rather than Iris being in therapy. Iris, a middle schooler, was suddenly experiencing extreme rage when things did not go her way.

I ruled out any past trauma as an explanation for her rage, or parenting issues. I quickly realized that Iris was experiencing trauma to the nervous system. She was an avid screen user and a junk food junkie addicted to sugar. She raged anytime her parents placed a boundary or said no to her. Her mother reported at times her rage could last for hours and consisted of such acts as throwing things, violent behavior toward her siblings, and vandalizing property.

If I were to diagnose her, I would say she had anxiety, oppositional defiant disorder, and ADD. I didn't diagnose her; I knew it wasn't a therapy issue. Therapy was only perpetuating Iris's shame. When she came in, her mother would report the episodes and Iris would vehemently argue and say, "I didn't say that" or "I didn't do that." She could not acknowledge her awful behavior because it was too painful. She had no interest in participating in therapy. I could talk to her from here until kingdom come, teach her how to recognize her feelings, express them appropriately, and learn to tolerate her discomfort. She was not going to respond well to that, and her parents and the whole family would suffer as a result. Her siblings were starting to be affected by her rageful episodes. I explained to her parents that because of her extreme reactions, I knew she was stuck in fight or flight. Her physiology was not allowing her nervous system to calm. This was likely due to gut and brain inflammation.

I explained this was not a therapy issue but a physiological issue and referred Iris to a functional medicine doctor. I then offered that I could be a support to her parents and Iris after she sought medical treatment for her stress. Her mother called six months later to report that things had improved immensely for Iris, and they were no longer in need of therapy services. Iris's family could begin to heal. They were no longer resentful of her behavior. They understood it and all rallied around her to help.

> **Avoiding problems you need to face is avoiding the life you need to live.**
> —*Paulo Coelho*

You are disconnected. Disconnected from yourself and your children. Dissociating is a subconscious reaction to your discomfort. This is your body's protection mechanism. Instinctual avoidance protects you from pain. What we avoid remains the same. It's no wonder parents are afraid to allow their children independence and freedom. To make them uncomfortable. To allow them to have their negative feelings without trying to control and fix it. You check out. You binge-watch TV, drink too much, smoke marijuana, scroll mindlessly on social media to calm your nervous system—only to feel worse because it's not doing the trick. What we avoid amplifies. Some of you are turning to pharmaceuticals because that seems like a better alternative to self-medicating. Everyone perpetually in a state of survival.

That thing you are dissociating from? It's not going away. It stays, festers under the surface, and causes all sorts of illness. Physical, mental, spiritual. We avoid because it's a stress response. A way to survive. Our bodies are made to survive threat. Dr. Andrew Neville, a chronic stress specialist, says that if a tiger is chasing you, you need the sympathetic nervous system. You also need the vagus nerve to help you rest and digest so you are not always in survival mode. This is what is missing for today's parents and children. We don't rest enough. We are surviving, not thriving. We don't stop from the mindless distractions with technology and take time to come down from the constant barrage of overstimulation. A movement to unplug for a day, a week, a month isn't enough. It's like a diet. It doesn't work. We must have a major lifestyle change to stop disconnecting and be with ourselves and our children.

What can parents do to foster a healthy family life?

Ask yourself, *What can I do today to make this change?* It can be as small as no devices at the dinner table. Turn off devices at least one hour before bedtime, play a family game, and go to bed early. Go for a walk, cook dinner together, plant a garden over the weekend. Be in nature, get fresh air, even if you live in a cold state like me! This will reset the nervous system, feel good, and encourage you to keep going. A heathy lifestyle takes time; it's small steps every day that add up to feeling better. American families can use more simplicity. Parents, it's OK to say no to the travel team or the "one more" activity. If you slow down, your children will feel that and slow down themselves. Once you feel better you will never want to go back to mindlessly scrolling, fear-based media, dissociating from streaming TV, family fighting because everyone's nervous systems are heightening, and disconnected relationships.

Put down your devices! The most disturbing image to watch is a parent locked on their screen while their child desperately tries to get their attention. You've seen it, you've done it, you've been that parent. I have too. I am cognizant of this every day and regret the times in the past I wasn't. Your children want to be with you. You are one of their favorite people. You are their center, their home. Even as they separate with each developmental phase, you will still be home base. You are enough for them. With all your imperfections and mistakes, they are built to survive them. I believe children's souls choose their parents. We are all here to learn something. They choose you to teach them.

KEY TAKEAWAYS

- ► Nutrition is foundational for a developing child.
- ► Parents should be aware that every major industry is targeting children as a marketing strategy and is not concerned about their overall health.
- ► Parents set the tone for emotion regulation.
- ► You can have a calm family by changing the family system bit by bit and creating more simplicity.

CHAPTER 4

COGNITIVE DEVELOPMENT

If you want your children to be intelligent, read them fairy tales. If you want them to be more intelligent, read them more fairy tales.

—Albert Einstein

The next developmental task in the four elements is cognitive development. If movement goes well, the brain is scaffolded (meaning the brain is protected and can develop the way it needs to) and ready for brain growth. This opens neuropathways, enabling children to experience the stages of cognitive development. This is how children learn as they relate to the world around them. Fully 90 percent of cognitive (brain) development occurs before the age of six. The remaining 10 percent takes place in the prefrontal lobe of the brain—responsible for executive functioning, impulse control, decision-making, and emotional regulation—and doesn't fully develop until a child is twenty-five. It's important we understand how the brain develops at various ages so we can have appropriate expectations of our kids at the right time in life.

According to board-certified pediatrician and adolescent coach Miriam Mandel, MD, "The brain's job is to interpret and create meaning between the inside world and the outside world. This is an important concept to know because brainwaves play a huge part in this dynamic. The brain processes over 10 million bits of information per second but can only consciously handle 40–50 per second."[19]

The following are four stages of cognitive development theorized by Jean Piaget.

Sensorimotor stage (birth-2)

The first stage is called the sensorimotor stage. Children at this age understand the world through senses and actions. Through real-world sensory stimulation. During this time children understand the world through sensory experiences of seeing, hearing, reaching, touching. A major milestone in this stage is what's called "object permanence."[20] This is when a child learns that an object exists without being seen. This helps them to develop a sense of self in relation to the world around them. Many babies have separation anxiety during this phase of development while they form their sense of their parent or caregiver returning after they leave the room. I recall my children crying when I walked away from them, many times simply to get something for them to eat. I would talk to them the whole time, reassuring that I was going to come back and explaining what I was doing. That's how they come out of object permanence without anxiety. A little separation anxiety is normal. It's important that parents stay present, allow children to play and explore, and engage and play with their children during this time so they come out of this stage grounded in trusting their caregiver. Imagine if a parent is on a digital smart device chronically during this time or if a toddler is given their own smart device. The lack of interaction would impede the exploration of the child's sensory development. This exploration is important for their brains to enter the next stage of cognitive development.

Many children today are being exposed to screens for what is considered educational purposes such as apps that boast teaching your two-year-old to read. A popular YouTube personality markets herself to parents of babies and toddlers to promote learning videos. But babies and toddlers don't need to be on a device to learn. There is no benefit for them to have tablets at this age. These products are peddled to parents touting that your child will "learn" using their devices and apps. A child learns through play, exploration, and the ability to use their imaginations.

I coach a set of parents for their eldest child. They bring their one-year-old to the sessions, and I have gotten to know her well; I will call her Mary. Mary is a typical one-year-old who terrorizes my office, then falls asleep at the end of the session just when it's time to go! She's extremely expressive and communicative. She babbles and says a handful of words but isn't talking in full sentences. Her mother, I will call her Ellen, asked me if she should be concerned about Mary's speech. My gut reaction was that Mary was fine, but I asked why before I responded. Ellen said people in her life were telling her they thought Mary should be talking by now. She said her older three kids were talking at this age. I don't expect kids to be talking in full sentences until they're closer to age two, if not almost three. I answered her that I thought Mary is developing beautifully: she's communicating nonverbally, she smiles when prompted, is playful, gives eye contact, and babbles. Then Ellen thought about it and realized the people telling her Mary may be developmentally behind all have their kids learning from apps that teach language. Ellen acknowledged her older three were on apps as well. She made changes to Mary's development by limiting her access to screens after working with me.

Lots of connections began to be made from there. Ellen realized all three of her older children had sensory issues as well as behavioral issues, before making changes to their screen usage. We concluded that apps may encourage children to talk sooner but they are causing other issues. Mary will talk in due time and will not stay behind her peers as she will catch up to them eventually. More importantly, she will have gotten the richness that is human interaction. Her mother's voice reading to her, looking into her eyes, her older siblings playing with her and connecting. No online personality or app can ever replace that!

In addition to preventing sensorimotor development, screen time causes overstimulation in the nervous system due to the junk light. *Junk light* describes the blue, green, and violet light emitted from screens, and its name was coined by David Asprey to explain how synthetic light is affecting our health.[21] Overstimulation from nonnatural light is affecting baby and toddler sleep. Sleep is extremely important during this phase of development because, according to Dr. Mandel, "[Delta brain waves measure at] approximately .5-4 cycles per second. Infants from 0-2 years old are in delta and that is why they sleep so much and cannot stay awake very long without a nap."[22] If babies stay awake too much during this time, it takes them out of their natural state and can wire the brain for overstimulation.

> When children pretend, they're using their imaginations to move beyond the bounds of reality. A stick can be a magic wand. A sock can be a puppet. A small child can be a superhero.
>
> —*Mr. Rogers*

Preoperational (2-7 years)

The next phase is preoperational and covers a child's imaginative state. Children at these ages understand the world through language and mental images. During this time imaginative play is very important. Dr. Mandel states, "Theta [waves] (4-8 cycles per second) [are present] for kids 3-6, this is a phase of deep imagination. Alpha [waves] (8-13 cycles per second) [are present when] children are between the ages of 7 and 12 [and] are in the phase where pretend games are 'real,' like a tea party or riding a stick horse. To them, it is real."[23] Do you remember this time in your childhood? I do. My brothers and I would turn our Hot Wheels bikes upside down and move the peddles so the front wheel would turn. We pretended the turning wheel was making ice cream and would shout "ice cream for sale!" Another classic was pretending the dining room table was a car. We would sit under it, and someone would be in the driver's seat, the passenger seat, and the back seat. Kids who grew up before technology were bored and came up with all kinds of fun games. We had no choice—there wasn't anything else to do!

Imaginative play is the essence of childhood learning. Children become good at pretend play during this time while simultaneously thinking concretely about the world around them. This is a great time to read to your child, especially fairy tales. Allow them the opportunity to enter worlds that stimulate the imaginative part of the brain. It is recommended that you read fairy tales and leave the interpretation of the story up to the child. This stretches their minds to come to conclusions about themselves and the experiences around them. This is necessary because to them, the world is black and white. If you don't allow creative thought, they risk being locked into concrete thinking as they grow.

Another important part of childhood is play. It is through play that children learn how to relate to themselves and others. Many children today are given tablets during this phase of development. Tablets made for young children come in a variety of colorful protective cases with a pair of headsets to match. The use of a tablet deprives children of seeing, hearing, and touching in the real world. This creates missed opportunities to explore and increase their learning. It hinders brain development.

I see a lot of dysregulated children at this age. They aren't getting what they need, and their emotions are out of control. Symptoms include tantrums, anxiety, anger, lack of eye contact, and difficulty with social interaction. The screen infiltrates the brain's process and doesn't allow for imagination. Of course, it's not just what the screen is doing to the brain, it's also what the child is not doing because he's on the screen. He's not playing with other children and learning social skills, and he's not bored—a necessary opportunity to come up with imaginative creative thoughts. This will cause behavior issues in any child. I have had countless families remove technology from children's lives and see immediate results. In some cases, it really is that simple. We think that because everyone is using devices for children, it's OK. It's become normalized. It's the same way I view food. Kid food and kid tablets. Tablets have become an accessory to childhood. Imaginative play has been stunted because they didn't get the time to play, to learn to grow their brains.

Here's a phrase all children love to use, and all parents hate to hear: I'm bored. Boredom is a necessary part of childhood. One of my favorite responses to "I'm bored" is from my daughter's kindergarten teacher. When the kids would tell her that they were bored, she would say, "That's good; that means you're about to have a creative idea." Boredom is hard. It's uncomfortable. But it's in boredom that everything happens. When they are bored, children's nervous systems can calm, which allows the brain to function in all its parts. Child development doesn't change because a shiny toy shows up on the market. Don't allow your young children to be seduced by this. Give them a childhood free from tech. Let them grow and learn naturally!

Concrete operational (7-11 years)

If the preoperational stage goes well, a child can move into the concrete operational stage of development. They start to understand the world through logical reasoning and categories. They are still concrete in this stage but can connect more to analytical concepts. Academics begin to be more rigorous during this time as children are more capable of learning higher-thinking concepts. The expectation on children is that they are ready to learn. Many children are unsuccessful in school today because their bodies aren't set up to learn. Rudolph Steiner schools do not teach reading until the age of seven because of the philosophy that children's bodies and brains need to develop first. Children begin learning to read in first grade through daily exercises that engage the midline of the body. The exercises involve crossing their arms and legs at the same time. They also work on tracking, moving their eyes from left to right to train the eye to be ready for reading from the left side of the page to the right. Many Silicon Valley executives from companies such as eBay, Apple, Google, and Yahoo! send their children to these schools because they are technology-free. They use chalkboards, paper, and pencils to stimulate the brain for growth and learning. They report that screens inhibit child development.[24] Steve Jobs notoriously banned iPads from his home when his children were young, Bill Gates didn't give his children smart devices until they were older, and Mark Zuckerberg limits screen use for his children.

Some children are not developing physically due to tech and this is causing retained reflexes, brain inflammation, and a lack of proper brain development. As a result, school anxiety is rampant. My colleagues and I over the years have often talked about how our summer months are slow in the practices that see children. Children come to therapy during the school year because they have developed so much anxiety about school. They feel low self-worth and don't want to try to learn. The summer brings respite from these feelings of inadequacy.

If children aren't allowed imaginative play in the previous developmental phase, they have more trouble with logical thinking and struggle in school. Many children in the preoperational age range are being given unnecessary diagnoses of learning disabilities simply because they didn't get what they needed developmentally.

Dr. Delia McCabe, a neuroscientist, talks about children's brains not developing properly because of a childhood on screens.

> Think of spring in a garden, when whatever you plant has a greater chance of thriving versus when autumn descends. Spring is the garden's "window of opportunistic growth" because the ingredients required for optimal growth are available—sunshine, warmth, prepared soil and water, and a plant primed to thrive under those conditions. These windows of development can only be optimized when the environment is optimized. The brain doesn't get a "do-over" or "rewind" because these windows of opportunity do close. If the environment was not conducive and optimal for that specific stage of neural development and the child (brain) didn't receive the input required during that specific period, then the brain is comprised and unfortunately may be disadvantaged for life.[25]

Dr. McCabe's reference to windows of development is evident in recent research highlighting achievement gaps in education due to the COVID-19 lockdowns of 2020.[26] Many kids continue to be behind, specifically in math and reading. The gaps in achievement were present prior to 2020 but widened, remain, and in some states are worse today. Many children were put on devices during this time. Their parents were working and not able to monitor their device usage, so children distracted themselves from school to play games, search the Internet, and scroll on social media. I had countless reports of my child and teen clients in their beds with cameras turned off while they were supposed to be learning. My own child, in fifth grade at the time, found himself distracted by the Internet while his teacher talked. We were at a device-free school, so online learning was a foreign idea to all of us. Our children missed so much development during this time. The damage may be permanent if overuse of devices continues.

Formal operational (12 years and upward)

Lastly, Piaget's fourth phase of development is formal operational. This is the understanding of the world through hypothetical thinking and scientific reasoning. Kids at this age begin to learn critical thinking. They become more sophisticated and are apt to engage in adult conversation. Adolescents have a better understanding of logic, critical thinking, and abstract ideas. Adolescents and young adults are expected to be apt to solve problems. This is when beta waves are developing in the brain.

"Beta brain waves (13-50 cycles per second) are the beginning of the analytical mind, where kids can rebel or reject ideas," says Dr. Mandel. "This usually occurs around puberty. Beta is the most common adult awake state. It can be low, medium, or high. High is when we are in fight-or-flight, while low can be having a casual conversation with a friend."[27]

I have so many examples to give of how today's teenagers and young adults are not able to solve their own problems. I choose the following one because it's so poignant and is the most severe form of children not developing and experiencing dysfunction as a result. The reason for this is because not enough stages of development went well overall. Certainly, some things developed; otherwise, we would be seeing every child with dysfunction and disorder. We are creeping up to this being the majority, so it is time to pay attention and understand child development on all fronts so we can give our children and teenagers what they need when they need it.

One of my clients, a college student I will call Penelope, and I had been working on allowing herself to be uncomfortable and working through hard things. She was making progress because she was pushing herself out of her comfort zone. She had prevented herself from having life experiences that she wanted but felt she could never have. She attended college but struggled to function day to day without the help of her mother, who would call in the morning and make sure Penelope was up and ready for class so she wouldn't be late. Penelope had a lot of setbacks, but eventually she was able to get to class, complete her assignments, and work with her professors to catch up all on her own. She eventually got a job that allowed her to interface with customers, and this helped her social anxiety immensely.

We had been working together for quite some time when she shared the following story with me. She and a few of her roommates were out one night. The next day one of her roommates realized she'd left a personal item at a restaurant, and because of her phone anxiety she couldn't call the restaurant to inquire about the item. Penelope, who had been working on pushing through her discomfort, said she didn't want to call, but she felt that she wanted to help her friend, so she pushed herself to make the call. She was also the most capable because she had been working on herself. As she was describing the scenario, I thought, *My goodness, things have gotten bad for this generation of young people.* Making a phone call is hard for them—something so simple to most of us in older generations. I couldn't help but feel sad for today's young people because they didn't get what they needed. Obviously, they never needed to make phone calls because they have messaging apps and all kinds of social media to keep in touch with friends. They also have meal-delivery apps and shopping apps where they can press buttons, enter their payment information, and *voila!*, they have what they want immediately. They are developmentally stunted and immature and are having trouble functioning in the world. We should pay attention. Allowing for and teaching kids' necessary developmental tasks at the right ages is integral to their healthy development and well-being.

Many adolescents today are using artificial intelligence (AI) for their schoolwork. From writing papers to solving math problems, kids are not thinking for themselves. Teachers and administration are aware of this and have their ways of knowing when AI is used, but kids are savvy and avoid leaving red flags. Brain development is surely being stunted when developing minds can't develop. I am aware of this even in face-to-face interaction with my own kids. I catch myself telling them what to do or trying to solve their problem for them. I stop and say, "Sorry, what do you think?" Allowing children to work out their thoughts, solve their problems, and think critically are necessary during the last phase of cognitive development.

KEY TAKEAWAYS

▸ Brain development occurs in stages that build on the one before it.
▸ Screen usage during critical parts of development, particularly before age six, can fracture development of the brain.
▸ We must be concerned for the prefrontal lobe and critical thinking development.

CHAPTER 5

SOCIAL EMOTIONAL DEVELOPMENT

If you love somebody, let them go, for
if they return, they were always yours.
If they don't, they never were.[28]
—KAHLIL GIBRAN

TODAY'S CHILDREN ARE GROWING UP FASTER THAN ANY previous generation and are increasingly more immature at the same time. They're exposed to technology and media that are completely inappropriate for their young ages. Due to this, they are playing violent video games, watching pornography, and recording and watching real-time video of kids fighting at school. They have the ability to alter a photo to make oneself look better, known as "filters" on social media, and "influencers" who are not a good influence. As a culture, we have developed a high tolerance for this type of content. As a result of this high tolerance, children are being treated as if they are mature and "smart" for their age. This is not how children mature. They mature by going through developmental stages naturally. Child development is a process and works like the rungs of a ladder, each stage building on the one before it. If one rung, or stage, doesn't go well it makes the next stage harder to conquer, but not necessarily impossible. When too many rungs are missing it becomes impossible to get to the stage the child needs, even if they are the correct age. It can be tempting, like picking low-hanging fruit, to do developmental tasks for them. That's the easy way out. Remember, parenting is hard, that's how you know you're doing it right. Children want to grow up and be given permission to do adult activities.

A child's brain continues to develop through human connection and attachment. If movement and cognitive development went well, a child can move through the phases of psychosocial development. My work in this area is loosely based on developmental psychologist Erik Erikson's theory of psychosocial development. He was particularly interested in how a personality develops in the context of its society and culture. According to Erikson, the personality develops as it successfully resolves crises that are social in nature. These involve establishing a sense of trust in others, developing a sense of identity in society, and helping the next generation prepare for the future.[29]

Trust versus mistrust (birth-18 months)

In the early years, from birth to eighteen months, Erikson defines attachment, which he calls trust versus mistrust.[30] If this stage goes well, an infant's emotional needs are met, and they develop trust and a healthy attachment to their caregiver. Later in life they will trust others in their relationships. If a child's emotional needs are not met in this stage, they will be fearful of the world. This translates to anxiety. Meeting a baby's emotional needs involves not only responding to their cries, but also interacting with them when they are awake; for example, smiling, cooing, and talking are all ways we can interact with a baby. If their caregiver is distracted by a screen, many opportunities for connection are missed. This could lead to the infant developing a lack of trust in others. It's the same if the baby is given a screen in this stage; the missed opportunities for connection are endless.

From birth to eighteen months, babies are in the attachment phase. Babies cue their caregivers, usually through crying, when they have a need. It is important the caregiver responds to that need. If the need is met, the baby will develop trust and connection.

Babies need human interaction in the form of eye contact, positive facial expressions, and physical touch. In the "Still Face Experiment," Dr. Edward Tronick[31] demonstrates a baby's distress upon the mother having a still face and not interacting with her baby. In the beginning of the study the mother is cooing, smiling, and playing with her baby. The baby is responding by reflecting back to the mother. It is a beautiful dance of a mother/child interaction. This is what fosters bonding and attachment. Then, the mother is instructed to have a still face according to the experiment, and the baby tries to get her attention through more smiling and cooing. However, when the mother's face continues to be still the baby becomes distressed and begins to scream and eventually cry. When the mother begins interacting again, the baby calms. In today's terms, the still face can manifest in either the mother having a device between her and the baby or the baby having a device themselves. Devices in this stage of development prohibit a connection between baby and caregiver and can lead to a lack of attachment and trust.

In the attachment phase of development, you can never spoil a baby with too much love and nurturing. Spoiling occurs when parents take over childhood tasks, hindering children from achieving their developmental milestones appropriately. Many parents are being fed garbage advice about the "cry it out" method during this time. There are people who call themselves a "sleep concierge" for parents who want to sleep-train their babies. They coach you through letting your baby cry it out. Mothers are hiring coaches to redirect them from their instinct, which is to go to their baby and comfort her when she cries. This is born out of a desire for parents to get their babies to sleep through the night so the parents aren't exhausted the next day. I see the attraction; I remember the baby stage and it as hard indeed. But I have no regrets as I answered my babies' cries all through the night.

Remember, this builds attachment and trust. If you leave a baby to cry it out and self-soothe then you are denying the process of healthy attachment. We have it flipped. We think babies should self-soothe and older kids should be made to be comfortable. Parents want to avoid all pain and discomfort of natural child development later, but overall are OK with allowing their babies to cry it out. It doesn't make sense. Self-soothing and learning how to tolerate painful feelings and discomfort come later in development, in every stage after attachment—not in the attachment phase. The attachment phase is when babies are set up for secure attachment later in life.

Children today often face challenges when it comes to experiencing natural child development. Parents, in their desire to provide a comfortable life for their children, sometimes unintentionally hinder children's growth by shielding them from frustration. With the advancement in the age at which parents start families compared to previous generations, there is often more financial stability, allowing for an inclination to make life easier for their children. However, it's important to remember that just because we can offer such convenience, it doesn't necessarily mean we should.

What cries should be attended to and what should the baby learn to work through on its own?

If you respond to their cries, babies learn that their needs can be met through communication. Secure attachment is crucial for developing trust in relationships later in life. Since babies lack verbal communication skills, crying becomes their way of expressing their needs. It is vital for caregivers to meet these needs as a foundation for relationships later in life. However, it's essential to discern which cries should be attended to and which ones babies can learn to navigate independently. It is acceptable for babies to struggle through developmental milestones such as rolling over, crawling, and walking. If they emit grunts or whimpers during these moments, it is OK for them to work through their frustration. This process helps them develop resilience and tolerance for challenges. On the other hand, when parents intervene excessively, assisting with tasks and preventing natural struggles, children don't learn how to master tasks and feel capable.

Contrary to popular belief, the cry-it-out method is not synonymous with letting babies work through challenges independently. When babies are left to cry for extended periods, their distress escalates, fracturing their trust in having their needs met. As a result, both the baby and the parents experience the release of stress hormones such as cortisol and adrenaline. Over time, this can lead to a heightened fight-or-flight response, and the bond between parent and child may be strained, lacking the beneficial effects of oxytocin (the love hormone).

Autonomy versus shame and self-doubt (1 ½-3 years)

This is defined as self-control without a loss of confidence and is the age of one and a half to three years old. This stage is all about independence. You have all heard of the terrible twos, the age in which a child learns the word no. When my kids were this age, I had to remind myself that every time they said "no" it was healthy. It's how children assert their will and authority. It's hard for the parent but necessary for the child. "No" at this age means they are asserting their independence. They are telling us what they want, at times very loudly. This is a boundary. They are learning how to express and communicate their boundaries. My friend's daughter (I'll call her G) demonstrated this well when she was two and her parents took her to a preschool interview. They were anxious, as G is their eldest child, and they didn't know what to expect. Her mother prepared her by telling her to "just have fun." Much to her parents' dismay, during the interview, G started to pick her nose! Her mother, mortified, said "G, let me get you a tissue." G replied with a resounding "NO." She was determined to get that snot out, and nothing was going to stop her. She succeeded! Her quick-witted father recovered and said, "Well, she's persistent and independent." G ended up getting in.

Remember the sensorimotor stage of brain development? At two, children learn to individuate. If their brains can process object permanence, then by two they are right on schedule to begin seeing themselves as an individual. It is our job to help them express their feelings but give them rules and boundaries for them to feel safe. If we do this right, they will develop self-confidence; if we do this wrong, they will lack self-esteem. It is a very tricky stage, one in which I have struggled as a parent. It's a delicate balance of their boundary and yours. They can absolutely say "no," but often your "no" is necessary for their safety. As in, "No, you cannot run across the street by yourself." Their "no" should be accepted with limits. You can give choices during this time. Limit the choices to two, and this will prevent them from being overwhelmed and allow them to have some form of control over themselves. Your "no" should be respected as well. It's a dance. Your boundary and theirs. It's crucial because this is where they learn to have boundaries and respect other people's boundaries as well.

Play is such an important part of this stage of development. In addition to aiding in brain development, play is where children learn to have control over themselves—an important piece of development as they learn to relate to others. We can't control other people, only ourselves.

I made a mistake with my second child during this stage of development, and oh, boy, did she tell me! She was two, and we were discussing her Halloween costume. She said she wanted to be a princess, specifically a princess from the movie *Frozen*. At the time, I didn't know what I know now about fairy tales, and I was convinced that princesses were a bad influence on young girls. During most of my childhood I had low self-esteem, particularly around the way I looked. I was constantly comparing myself to models in magazines and actresses in movies I watched. I have since come to realize that a young girl's infatuation with princesses is natural and healthy. As a part of their imagination, fairy tales and princesses satiate their desire to learn about a world beyond themselves, so different from what they know. When she asked me to be a princess, I suggested that she be an animal instead, such as a cat or dog or monkey. She ended up being Olivia, the pig from the book series and TV show, and I was relieved when Halloween came and she hadn't fought me on the costume. She seemed happy with the choice. Until she was getting dressed. She said, "Mom, you should have let me be a princess." My heart sank. At such a young age she was cognizant of pleasing me over advocating for what she wanted. In my desperation to save her from having low self-esteem like me, I lost sight of who she really is.

A girl who likes to dress up and imagine she is in a magical world is completely normal at two, given it's the beginning of the imaginative part of brain development. It was then that I realized I needed to give her more independence and teach her how to speak up for things that she wanted. I started to see that her obsession with princesses was not something I could control. I surrendered. I let her explore. Now, at age ten, she is passionate about musical theater. She puts all her effort and work into singing, dancing, and performing in plays. She recently auditioned for a solo role, earned it, and performed in her choir concert. And the song was "Part of Your World" from *The Little Mermaid*. She rocked it and brought tears to my eyes. Her favorite songs to sing to this day are Disney songs! I'm so grateful that she was able to tell me what she needed, and I was able to listen.

Initiative versus guilt (3-5 years)

This is the age when children begin to interact with peers and continue to engage in make-believe play. Through play and peer interaction, a child learns initiative and develops a sense of purpose. They feel secure in their ability to interact with their peers and make decisions. It's important that parents allow their children independence and autonomy during this time. This helps build their sense of self and feelings of confidence. If autonomy is not encouraged during this phase of development either because of criticism or control from the parent, a child will develop a sense of guilt. They will feel as though they are an annoyance to others and become followers lacking in self-confidence.

If attachment and will and authority went well, then the child is able to learn independent tasks. Important in this stage is children doing tasks of daily living, such as dressing themselves—including buttoning their shirts, zipping up their coats, and tying their shoes—and learning how to be in the kitchen cooking alongside their parents. These tasks will be very frustrating for children in this age group. The bones in their hands are not fully fused until the age of six, but from an emotional stand-point they need to learn frustration tolerance. Tantrums are common among three- to five-year-olds because they lack the skills to work through discomfort and regulate themselves. Parents must teach regulation early to avoid ongoing tantrums in a child's later years. When children have a tantrum, parents become uncomfortable, likely because their feelings weren't met well when they had big feelings as a child. Many parents react to tantrums by ignoring or meeting the child's anger with more anger. I suggest being there for your child as they go through these big feelings. Ground yourself and stand strong. Whatever you need to do to show up is necessary, because you are creating the energy space. If they can melt down while you stand or sit next them, that makes them feel safe. Then you can aid in working through their feelings by asking your child how their body feels when they are upset.

Many children at this age don't have the vocabulary to explain feelings. They are learning so much, and we often overlook teaching them the words for how they feel. It's much easier and accessible for them to express how they feel inside. You can ask this of a child at any age, because vulnerability is difficult for everyone, but this age range is where it should start. Many kids will report their head, stomach, or chest will hurt. They may feel a knotted-up stomach or shortness of breath. Once you have asked them where they feel it and what the feeling is, it's much easier for them to find ways to manage it. You can ask them what they need to feel better—maybe a hug, a warm bath, or going for a walk. Giving them the tools allows them to have autonomy over themselves. Older kids can identify what they need so they don't feel they are being lectured or controlled. Ideally, starting from ages three to five will allow kids to recognize their feelings themselves as they grow, and they likely won't need help other than for you to listen and show up.

Typically, children at this age enter preschool. In many cases this is the first time they will interact with peers, teachers, and parents of their peers. The reason why it is so important that they learn and work through their frustration with activities of daily living is so that when they leave their parents, they will feel strong and capable. I am a stickler for shoe tying at this age. It's so important that children learn to work through their frustration because they come out the other side feeling good about themselves. This eliminates separation anxiety. Some kids experience separation anxiety because they are insecure in their attachment to a parent. This occurs in cases when parents aren't emotionally available or there is some form of abuse or neglect. However, most separation anxiety, in my experience, is not because of the latter. It's due to children not being ready to be away from their parents. They are unable to toilet on their own, zip up their coats, or open containers in their lunchbox. Many parents do these tasks for their children to avoid frustration and discomfort. Children are ready for school and separation from their parents when they feel competent doing things for themselves. I understand it is more convenient for you to get your child ready to go somewhere. Waiting for them to complete tasks requires you to allow more time to get to your destination. But I assure you, it's worth it. It won't take long before they are more independent, and this takes the load off you sooner. Instead of waiting for your five-year-old to learn to get out the door, can you imagine your three-year-old doing it? When a three-year-old can feel good about themselves in this way it translates into a five-year-old helping with younger siblings, a nine-year-old cooking dinner, and a sixteen-year-old driving. The sooner independence is taught, the less parents must do.

US surgeon general Dr. Vivek Murthy sounded the alarm on parent burnout and declared it a public-health issue. He asserted the parental load is overwhelming due to cultural parenting challenges such as children's health and safety, social media, and technology, as well as uncertainty about their futures. The Department of Health and Human Services reports that 48 percent of parents say they are completely overwhelmed by stress, compared to 26 percent among adults who are not parents.[32] I believe parent burnout is a result of parents doing too much for their children, starting as young as three. I think the reason for this is that parents feel they must accommodate their child's every desire. Giving them a happy childhood is at the top of the list. I wish for parents to know this: A happy child is one who can work through hard things, and a happy childhood is one that has hard things to work through.

During this stage, three- to five-year-old children need to be interacting with their peers and learning how to be social. If they are secure in themselves because they know how to do tasks of development, they will be secure in their interactions with others. They learn how to share, resolve conflict, and stand up for themselves when necessary. Unstructured play is necessary and integral during this time. This is how children learn to relate to one another. Adults should step in when necessary, in case conflict escalates.

Many parents think preschool is when children should be learning their ABCs and 123s. While they are capable of learning academics at this age, the richness of what they learn through unstructured, unsupervised play with their peers is far more valuable. Academics will come in due time when their brains are more ready for it. I particularly noticed the importance of social emotional learning during the fall and winter of 2022. I had gotten an influx of calls from parents of first-grade children (ages six and seven). Each new case seemed like the one before it. A child was experiencing anxiety and social issues during recess. The child was anxious overall, at times school avoidant, didn't want to separate from parents, and was finding recess troublesome because other kids were "being mean." I found that the "mean child" was simply not able to communicate effectively and needed to learn better social skills, and the child who was feeling "bullied" did not have confidence to stand up for themselves and communicate effectively either.

Why was I seeing this same issue over and over again? Those children were three, four, and five during the lockdowns. Some of them were online for preschool, others attended in person. The kids online were getting no benefit since learning at that age should all be through play and interactions. The kids who attended preschool in person were in masks and could not see one another's facial expressions or even hear tones of voice, since that was muffled and they had to keep their distance. They were not experiencing life in the real world. Many didn't have to do tasks of development such as tie their shoes, put coats on, or open lunch containers because they were isolated from the world. I saw so many deficits in the six-year-old children coming to me that year because of this. They hadn't completed autonomy and independence; they couldn't rely on themselves. Therefore, they were anxious and lacked social skills.

> **By overprotecting children, we are not protecting their childhoods.**

Play-based childhoods are being stolen from today's iGeneration. The lack of play early on is not allowing children to develop naturally and have a sense of independence, which causes anxiety. Anxiety among today's children has reached epidemic levels. By 2019, 9.4 percent of children aged three to seventeen in the US had anxiety, and those numbers have only increased since the 2020 lockdowns.[33] At its root, anxiety is about a loss of power and control over oneself. Many children labeled with an anxiety disorder today are struggling with an inherent lack of trust in themselves. This makes them feel out of control and as a result, they hyperfocus on something outside of themselves to control. Play fosters all that good learning and gives young children control over themselves, which is the foundation for trusting themselves later.

Competence versus inferiority (5-12 years)

Erikson defines the period from ages five to twelve as "industry,"[34] otherwise known as competence versus inferiority. He theorizes that children of this age are gaining confidence through their ability to discover likes and interests on their own. If they are successful, they feel confident. If they are unsuccessful, they feel inferior. If a child feels inferior, they lack self-esteem.

Our culture, so obsessed with safety, is preventing children from gaining confidence and self-assuredness. We aren't allowing them the opportunity to get hurt, to get dirty, to be free, to have experiences that allow them to fail. Children at this stage of development do not build confidence from winning awards or getting good grades. That's a bonus. Confidence comes from doing hard things—working through them and coming out the other side, feeling strong, capable, and ready to do it again. This is when you can say, "Wow, look at me, I did it." Failure is necessary because it teaches you how to learn from your mistakes and how to tolerate disappointment and pain. This is a part of life. It cannot be avoided. Many kids at this age don't try to challenge themselves due to a fear of failure. Parents model a play-it-safe mentality, and kids follow suit.

In Steiner schools, kindergarteners learn to prepare their shared snack every day. Part of this food preparation includes using knives. The first time I entered a Steiner school I saw twenty five- and six-year-olds cutting up vegetables with adult knives to put in their soup, their snack for the day. Healthy food is also part of the culture of the school, and parents are encouraged to pack lunches with whole, nutritious foods. I will never forget how amazed these children were to be allowed to use knives! How they all were trusted with a dangerous object and were totally under control independently. Every one of them exuded confidence and certainty about their ability to do the job they were given. The adults trusted them; therefore, they trusted themselves. Later I learned how what I saw came to be. The children learn how to use a knife safely by watching the adults first, doing it with supervision, and finally feeling ready to use knives independently. The amount of control the classroom was kept under had nothing to do with the teacher and everything to do with the fact that the children could keep themselves under control because they were learning how to do something hard.

During this phase of development, many kids are on social media, playing games, and using apps that prevent them from experiencing life. There is life all around us. The simple moments like the one I described encapsulate so much meaning. If kids are looking down at a screen, they will miss life. They will miss opportunities to challenge themselves to stretch out of their comfort zone and to be proud of themselves and have a sense of accomplishment. Many kids in this age group develop a foundation for being purposeless later. Many of today's adolescents and young adults struggle to find meaning in their lives. It starts in these years when kids should be working on building themselves with the encouragement and trust of the adults in their lives. Child development builds. You can't have the cherry on top unless you've worked to make the sundae. Otherwise, there won't be anything to put the cherry on top of. The parts of the proverbial sundae are all the intricacies of day-to-day life, the interactions we face just by stepping out of our homes.

The challenge of a child getting up in the morning, getting ready for school, remembering to bring their soccer shoes for after-school practice and being on time, showing up, focusing, being respectful, and managing social interactions—these are challenging to children. I see parents making sure their kids are up and out of bed (I am guilty of this, too, but I'm working on it), packing their lunches for them, noticing they forgot their soccer shoes and bringing them to the school so they won't have to run laps per the coach's consequence. Parents are doing tasks of development for their children. If kids can do it for themselves, even when it's hard, especially when it's hard, they can feel good and have a true sense of confidence and self-trust. Parents can work through your natural tendencies to want to do things for your children and take a step back. Allow them to try it. If they fail, it's OK; they will learn from it, and you will too.

Ego identity versus role confusion stage (12-18 years)

If the prior development stage went well, a child leaves with confidence and is ready for identity development. This is a critical time, as one is transitioning from childhood to adulthood. During this time, the teen becomes more independent and begins to look to the future in terms of education and what they want to do for their career. What is also happening is a desperate need to fit in and belong. While wanting to fit in, a teenager also wants to assert independence and is developing her identity. The teenager is learning the roles he will occupy as an adult. The teenager is reexamining her identity and trying to find out who she is. At this stage, the teen is exploring their emotional identity. What should happen at the end of this stage, if everything goes well, is a strong sense of self. If this does not go well, a teen is often influenced by peer pressure. This is when we see teens involved with excessive drinking, drug use, and promiscuous sexual behavior. If the teen does not have a strong sense of self, he or she will engage in what others are doing and what might seem cool to peers. In terms of screens, when a teen does not have a sense of self, he or she engages in an online facade of being someone that they are not. The screen is an easy modality to avoid all issues the child is facing. It's an escape into a world where they are in control.

An example of this online facade is the selfie. The goal of a selfie is to demonstrate perfection. The selfie is very important because this feeds into the online facade. If you look perfect in your selfie, your peers will view *you* as perfect in the real world, even if behind your selfie is a lack of self-confidence. The perfect selfie is one in which the angle is flattering to the body, and the teen is made up and dressed in a very sexy way. Often girls exhibit "duck lips" to look sexy. Many teens do not have a good understanding of sex and sexuality but are engaging in sexually suggestive poses to seem cool and appear to be more mature than they are. Girls seek attention through their physical appearance, while boys seek attention through competition. Girls are more vulnerable than boys to the oversexualization social media creates. And online gaming is more addictive for boys than girls.

A teen's sexual development is occurring during this stage as well. They can become self-conscious of their bodies. Erikson asserts that the adolescent may feel uncomfortable about their body for a while until they can adapt to the changes.[35] The selfie portrays confidence but what's behind it is the opposite. Ideally a child should obtain the virtue of fidelity during this time. Fidelity involves being able to commit oneself to others based on accepting others, even when they may have ideological differences. Many young people today are not developing fidelity because of cancel culture and social media algorithms feeding us only one side, giving us what we want to keep us coming back. If I am unable to stand in the acceptance of myself, I cannot accept others. It's starts with the "I," and it's painful. Working through the uncertainty of identity development, who you are as a person, is hard. The ability to unfriend, ghost, and otherwise shut out someone with an opposing view is available to this generation. Previous generations had to work through this because cancelling friends, family, and public figures was not easy. During this stage, it feels like a threat when someone has ideological differences because your own thoughts and feelings are just starting to develop. To control those unresolved emotional issues, young people become protective of those feelings and avoid them. Avoiding the pain leads to low self-esteem, depression, and anxiety.

This phase allows the child to explore possibilities and begin to form their own identity based upon the outcome of their explorations. Failure to establish a sense of identity within society can translate into something as simple as, "I don't know what I want to be when I grow up," to something as complicated as confusion about how they identify themselves. Today's children are told they can be anything they want. They can even be an animal, as evidenced by "furry culture." This is an online culture of people who identify as animals and mythical, fantasy creatures. Many young people who are socially awkward and do not have many friends tend to gravitate toward these online forums. The pull for these young people is a sense of belongingness. Parents and schools are affirming children when they say they identify as animals and allowing them to remain in their delusions. Role confusion involves an individual not being sure about themselves or their place in society. In response to role confusion or identity crisis, an adolescent may begin to experiment with different lifestyles (e.g., the way they dress and other specific appearances).

Exploration with a non-affirming professional therapist is the best way to treat these issues. This type of treatment will allow a child to work through their discomfort with identity development. The majority of children make their way out of confusion once allowed to explore the deeper issues behind it.

Overuse of technology can affect growth in an adolescent exploring their identity. Years ago, I received a call from a worried father regarding his fourteen-year-old son, who had told his parents that he wanted to meet a stranger he'd met online who lived in another country. This child, an avid online video gamer, was allowed unfettered access to games with no time limits. He'd met someone through the game and developed a relationship. This person invited the child to visit him overseas. The father reported that this boy identified as a furry and the parents affirmed his identity. They didn't find anything amiss with his furry identity, becoming alarmed only when he wanted to leave the country to meet a stranger. I explained to the father in the first call that the gaming, furry identification, and meeting a stranger were all in the category of immaturity due to an excessive use of technology. I assured the father this is something I could help with, but they would need to make changes to their son's lifestyle. The goal would be to help him socialize in the real world. The father said his son had trouble socializing and he was more comfortable online. I stressed that it was important he work through his discomfort because being online wasn't safe.

The referral came from a pediatrician who called me after I spoke with the father. She said he had decided to go with another therapist who affirmed their son. This boy was psychologically damaged, and his growth was stunted. The person trying to get him to come visit was likely a predator or sex trafficker. Many children are susceptible to online grooming. Grooming is a form of manipulation predators use to coerce children into sex acts. They befriend, pretend to be the child's age, give them compliments, and then plan to meet up, often asking for nude photos of the child to desensitize them to sex acts.

Parents, I recommend setting limits on your child's screen time early in this stage of development. They are heavily influenced by exposure to media during this time. You as the parent want to be more of an influence on them than anyone else. Your guidance and wisdom are what they need.

Intimacy versus isolation (18-25 years)

Young adults need to form intimate, loving relationships with other people. The alternative is loneliness. Today's young adults are struggling to find meaning in their lives, connect to themselves, and be healthy. If they don't have access to themselves, they cannot possibly have access to connect to anyone else. They have been told that their economic futures are bleak, and many of them are choosing not to have children because they don't want to raise them with all of today's problems. This despair affected by media sells fear. They were raised on social media that promised them they would be the most connected generation ever. Instead, they are more disconnected, disordered, and dysfunctional than any generation before them. Generation Z (born between 1997 and 2012) is the lost generation. If I were to describe them in one phrase it would be, "I don't want to grow up, and you can't make me."

Many of them lack the ability to form basic social connections. They don't look you in the eye, they have anxiety talking to strangers, and they can't make phone calls. Many of them can't order off a menu because they grew up pressing a button and having food delivered right to their door. They don't have the proper foundation to build strong, loving, intimate relationships, so they are lonely. They are angry, and rightfully so; their childhood was stolen from them. My message to them and my message to you as their parents is that *no one is a victim.* The wound may not be their fault, but it is their responsibility. It is your responsibility as their parents to let them go, giving them the independence they need to navigate the world.

I am astonished at how many parents are involved in their adult children's lives to an extent that doesn't allow for independence. I've seen countless adult children in my practice who can't even get through the day without calling their parents multiple times to ask for advice or help to solve a problem that they should be capable of solving themselves at their age. This should be the end of their childhood. This should be a time when they take responsibility for themselves, when they form relationships outside of their parents. Separation is important; parents grow old and eventually die. If adult children don't separate, they struggle with letting go of their parents. They shouldn't need parents anymore. That's not to say parents can't be close to their adult children but there's a time for separation and a time when parents and children can finally be friends. The job of parenthood is complete.

This is preventing them from growing up and from having families of their own. Using discernment to know that the circle of life must continue no matter what the fearmongering media say. I see many young adults who are afraid to date. They don't want to get hurt or be vulnerable. They use dating apps to protect themselves from having to form lasting, loving relationships because that's scary. Once you love someone, then you have something to lose, and since they developed without tolerance for their pain, they prefer to avoid loss and be lonely rather than to take risks and get hurt.

Do you remember when Berger broke up with Carrie Bradshaw (the main character on the popular TV show *Sex and the City*) with a Post-it note? I know only the women might remember this! And if the men remember, they may not be willing to admit it! But if you haven't seen this episode, here's some context. Carrie's boyfriend broke up with her on a Post-it that read, "I'm sorry, I can't, don't hate me."

The rest of the show, Carrie and her girlfriends lamented how horrible of a person he was for not being man enough to break up in person. Carrie even avoided being arrested for marijuana possession because she showed the police officers the note and they felt so bad for her, they let her go.

I thought of this recently as I continue to hear about breakups among Generation Z over text. At least Berger had the decency to write something with his own hand, not type behind a screen. Today, text breakups are considered normal. Nothing wrong with them, no harm done. However, the emotional harm is being done in a way Gen Z doesn't understand because it's so normal to them. Fewer than twenty years ago it was abhorrent to think that it would be OK to break up with anyone other than in person. Now, it's perfectly OK to do so over text.

How did we get here? The screen is a barrier to real human interaction. Generation Z is being raised without facial expressions, tones of voice, body language, and eye contact. This erodes empathy and causes someone to disconnect from the human side of interpersonal relationship.

Studies of babies show that facial expression and body language help regulate their feelings. Due to interpersonal relationships lacking empathy and real human interaction, Gen Z has developed a fear of abandonment and trouble regulating that fear.

If a breakup is so easy, just type a message and you're done, then it can be done at any time, any way, out of the blue, on a whim. So many young people of this generation, terrified of a breakup, obsess over doing everything right. They lack communication skills to talk in person or even on the phone. This causes a lot of misconceptions and miscommunications among them. Conflict resolution is not developing due to this lack of communication.

Many of the relationship issues I hear about can easily be remedied with proper communication, expression of feelings, and the tolerance for potential conflict.

Parents can help by talking to their kids about their relationships. Stay connected to them and model what a healthy connection looks like. Teach them interpersonal skills that we take for granted but which this generation is lacking. Show them how to have uncomfortable conversations and work through conflict. Teach them how to call on the phone and talk, how to order off a menu instead of using food delivery apps. Using these apps prevents one from having to have any human interaction. You don't even have to answer the door; the driver simply leaves the food on your doorstep. Ask your children to buy your groceries to go through the process from start to finish. These are simple independent tasks that we don't think we have to teach our kids, but they never learned like we did. Most importantly, parents can help encourage their children to talk to their friends and significant others in person as much as possible. Human connection does not happen virtually!

KEY TAKEAWAYS

- ► We need to protect social emotional development.
- ► Understand what children need developmentally and provide that for them.
- ► Allow them to work through discomfort; growing is hard, and it's good to do hard things.

Call to Action

If you haven't already, be sure to download the *Free to Fly Kit* by going to the website https://nicole-runyon. mykajabi.com/-bonus-material or scanning the QR code below.

There you will find a hidden bonus to help you with the chapter you just read. Simply enter your name and email to receive the kit. Then take the *How Independent Are Your Children?* assessment to help you determine what tasks are appropriate for your kids at their current ages.

CHAPTER 6

GENDER DYSPHORIA

It is worth asking whether a
standard guided less by biology
than by political correctness is in
the best interest of patients.
—ABIGAIL SHRIER, IRREVERSIBLE
DAMAGE: THE TRANSGENDER CRAZE
SEDUCING OUR DAUGHTERS

IDEOLOGY, PARTICULARLY GENDER IDEOLOGY, HAS TAKEN over our culture.

Teenagers in this stage of development are naturally going to be self-conscious about their bodies. They are uncomfortable as they go through puberty; it's always an awkward stage. I'm sure all of us can remember just how hard this time was although it's a necessary time.

All adolescents must go through this and learn to work through their discomfort.

Many children today are turning to online forums in which influencers talk about gender transition. Kids who feel uncomfortable in their bodies find solace in this information. A "simple" fix for their complex problem. Algorithms on social media feed depressed children and teens information about gender dysphoria, pushing videos of influencers promising transitioning will solve all their problems, and planting in their head that transitioning their gender is the only way out of their discomfort. The kids share this information with their parents, who often don't know what to do. They go to trusted medical professionals who should not be trusted. "Affirming care," as it's called, is damaging to children and families, as therapists and doctors tell parents that their children will die by suicide if they don't transition. They ask parents, "Would you rather have a dead daughter or a live son?" Parents desperate to make sure their child doesn't die enter the child, whose brain isn't fully developed, into a medical system that immediately begins their transition. Vulnerable families are manipulated and pressured into a lifelong decision that cannot be reversed. Children as young as thirteen are allowed to make these decisions on their own without parental consent in some states. The "gender-affirming" therapist, only there to support the transition, does nothing to help the confused child sort through their feelings of pain. Gender-affirming care in therapy entails referring the child to medical transition and "emotionally supporting" him/her while undergoing treatment. No evaluation, no exploration for root causes of the gender-identity crisis.

Gender dysphoria in children is a psychological diagnosis in which a child who is born as one gender desires to be another gender. The child believes they are in the wrong body and desires to have a different one. They have a strong dislike for their body. They prefer cross-dressing and demonstrate a desire for such things as toys, activities, and games typically slated for the opposite sex. Many parents, therapists, and doctors are allowing children as young as three and four to identify as the opposite gender in which they are born. These children simply could have an opposite-sex sibling and playmate who is influencing their preferences in activities, toys, and games.

For example, a boy with an older sister who plays dress-up and paints his nails. This certainly does not mean he is gender dysphoric and should be transitioned. My daughter grew up with an older brother and boy cousins. When she was two, we were swimming with cousins at their grandparents' house. The boys were getting out of the pool and urinating in the bushes because they could! She tried to do the same, and quickly realized she didn't have the same parts. I told her we had to go inside and use the toilet. The entire time we were walking to the bathroom she was crying and shouting, "I want to be a boy!" That certainly doesn't mean she should have been treated as a boy; she was only trying to say, "I don't want to have to go inside and miss all the fun." I think many parents are confused by how to treat these situations. There are many parents who allow their very young children to choose their gender, but this can be confusing and extremely damaging to a developing child.

Diagnoses for youth gender dysphoria in the US have seen a large increase. In 2015, 15,172 children were diagnosed. By 2021, that number had risen to a staggering 42,167.[36] Due to the gender-affirming care narrative from the medical system, children are suffering from confusion and a lack of professional support. The pharmaceutical industry stands to make large amounts of money on children medically transitioning genders, as they will be on hormone drugs for a lifetime. Overall, the sex-reassignment surgery market stands to make $3.1 billion by the end of 2036.[37] These projections are due to the massive increase in gender dysphoria diagnoses. The push for gender-affirming care has ties to a potentially billion-dollar industry. Gender-affirming care immediately places children as young as eight on puberty blockers if they have not gone through puberty yet. Subsequently, they are given cross-sex hormones, and finally undergo surgeries such as mastectomies (removal of breasts), vaginoplasty (construction of a vagina), and phalloplasty (construction of a penis). Boys who endure vaginoplasty surgery must "dilate" for the rest of their lives. This requires placing a round instrument into the constructed vagina to hold its shape. It must be done multiple times per day for the first year, then weekly. It can be painful and emotionally exhausting.[38] The puberty blocker and cross-sex hormone drugs alone have lasting impacts on children's health, including infertility.[39] Side effects to these drugs include high blood pressure, high cholesterol, weight gain, sleep apnea, and blood clots.[40] Cross-sex hormone therapy can also have cardiovascular risk and bone-health issues.[41]

Many of these gender dysphoric children have been physically, mentally, and sexually abused, their underlying trauma causing depression and anxiety. Online forums give them a way out of their misery, their peers promising relief from the way they feel about their bodies. Anther phenomenon is that children, adolescents, and young adults on the autism spectrum are vulnerable to gender confusion. One study found that children with autism spectrum disorder (ASD) were four times more likely to experience gender dysphoria over matched controls of other groups of children.[42] Children with ASD struggle with social skills and feel more comfortable online. I was trained to aid children with autism in learning healthy social skills, even when doing so caused discomfort. I helped these children work through those feelings rather than avoid them. I don't see that happening today. The narrative has shifted, and therapists encourage comfort over challenges. It's more comforting for a child with autism to interact online than in real life. However, they are being manipulated online to transition genders, leaving them confused.

In 2017 the Gender Identity Development Service (GIDS), also known as The Tavistock Centre, in London saw a 5,000 percent increase in gender dysphoria among teenage girls in seven years. (Yes: 5,000!) The clinic has been shut down since it became an NHS service in 2009, the result of whistleblowers reporting that GIDS was rapidly transitioning young people before exploring the underlying root causes for their dysphoria. It was discovered that many of the girls had underlying mental health conditions that were not being addressed by the clinic. They were put on puberty blockers and began medical transition after merely two sessions with therapists on staff.[43] What ensued was more than one thousand children were given puberty blockers.[44] In her book *Time to Think: The Inside Story of the Collapse of the Tavistock's Gender Service for Children*, Hannah Barnes details what went wrong, chronicling the unethical practices that were not rooted in the best interests of children. It's a cautionary tale, one we should all be aware of, because in the name of virtue signaling and kindness, we are missing a very important opportunity to help children either work through gender-identity issues or prevent them altogether.

I believe the reason for such rapid-onset gender dysphoria with girls has roots in social contagion. Not only are children being seduced by influencers online, but there are transgender groups in real life that offer belonging and friendship. Girls fall into the trap of social media more often than boys and form friend groups in order to belong, whereas boys will stay lonely if they don't feel they belong. These are cliques—groups of friends who identify as the same. Belongingness in middle and high school is vital for adolescents who are trying to find themselves and relate to others at the same time. Identity development can feel like a toddler learning to walk: unstable and wobbly, falling often. A tumultuous time is made more comfortable by a group that accepts you. This can give solace to a teen who is feeling unsure of themselves. Inherently, friend groups are a great way to connect to peers. People just like you make you feel that you are OK in the world. Adults do the same thing. We have our work friends, our old friends, and perhaps new parent friends from our kids' social lives. The problem isn't the cliques in transgender groups. The problem is that the connection with the group requires you to identify as someone other than yourself. This puts pressure on kids to try and be something they are not, which is something cliques have done since the beginning of time.

How gender dysphoria affects boys

Boys are struggling because there is still a stigma to talking about their feelings, so they are not asking for therapy or going to therapy willingly when parents require it, compared to girls who are affected by the social contagion of mental illness on social media. I have seen many boys come into my office resistant, and it simply doesn't work. Parents, you can help your boys. They don't need to be pushed into therapy; there is another way. Gender dysphoria is a complex, multifaceted issue. In addition to the root cause explanations I've noted, I want to highlight a deeper issue many boys are experiencing, one that isn't on the surface. We don't see it because it isn't so obvious. Boys internalize negative feelings about being boys. Our culture is not particularly kind to them (nor is it kind to men). Men are considered toxic, their masculinity shamed. Boys see this and are shameful about their gender.

Many boys are not growing up. I hear from parents that their boys are generally forgetful, disorganized, lacking attention and focus, unmotivated, and apathetic. The number of men enrolled in college has fallen behind women in record levels. Women make up 59.5 percent of college students compared to 40.5 percent of men.[45] Boys are experiencing a failure to launch. They lack purpose and meaning in their lives. They are increasingly lonely, lethargic, depressed, anxious, and abusing substances.

Boys die by suicide at three to four times the rate of girls. That rate has been rising since 2006.[46] Early on, boys are not encouraged to be themselves. Taught to suppress their natural tendencies, they are overwhelmingly overdiagnosed with ADD/ADHD. I have become accustomed to saying to parents when they question whether their son has ADD/ADHD that "ADD = boy." Most boys are hyperactive and inattentive. They love to run, jump, play, be competitive, and wrestle with one another. It's their nature; it's who they are. If a boy is not this, he is the exception and not the rule. School does not allow for the level of play and physical activity boys need. They are expected to sit still, pay attention, and keep themselves under control. They don't get nearly enough time for recess to get their energy out and are often targeted by their teachers as "trouble."

Why are we putting boys in environments they don't thrive in and then pathologizing them with a diagnosis? So many boys think something is wrong with them because they can't sit like girls in school, pay attention, and please their teachers. They become labeled when they are young. The shame is too painful to acknowledge, so their brains are forced to "go somewhere else." So they show more executive-functioning issues that fit the criteria for ADD such as more disruptive behavior. Faced with pressure from the school, parents turn to stimulant drugs because they don't know how to help. This is causing depression and, because boys don't feel that expressing and communicating feelings is strong or "manly," their depression goes untreated. Boys need to know that being vulnerable *is* being strong—it's the hardest thing you can do.

Boys have a proclivity for being active and physical. When my son was in his toddler years, we barely went anywhere he couldn't run! I remember taking him to open fields regularly just to let him run and use his energy in a positive way. We lived in another state for a year when he was one, and I remember those long flights home being so hard with an active one-year-old boy. I think I wore out the airplane aisle walking him up and down! This doesn't mean boys cannot and should not learn how to sit, be quiet, and be respectful in public. It just means we must have more patience teaching them to do so. They feel the energy from the adults around them and pick up on it early. Therefore, they may develop a feeling that they are bad, a disappointment to adults. They are told, even nonverbally, that they are a nuisance. Then they become that. It's a self-fulfilling prophecy.

I have a friend who has two girls and another friend who has two boys. My friend with the girls and I went to visit our friend with the boys (who were six and four at the time) for a weekend. They were being boys and took the cushions off the couch, were jumping, and being wild! Having a boy myself, I didn't think anything of it and continued talking as if we were not in a room with boys jumping. My friend with girls was shocked and not able to continue the conversation. She stopped at one point, looking bewildered, and said, "They are jumping!" I laughed and said, "Yeah, they are boys!"

I remembered that she and I had each been pregnant with our second child, and hers was born first. I came over to help her with her oldest (girl) while she slept, and my son was at school. I was amazed at how her daughter was able to sit and color for two hours! I was lucky to get five minutes out of my son to sit still. When she was later shocked about the boys jumping, I recalled that time I'd spent with her daughter coloring and listening to classical music. How different that was from what I knew!

Boys are not bad, they are not defined by ADD/ADHD, they are not a nuisance. We must allow boys to be themselves. They don't need therapy—they need you. Remember, boys need to feel strong and capable. Being strong is necessary. We need boys to become men who can protect and fight if they need to, so they don't fight when they feel their ego is threatened. That's foundational for their psychological well-being. Let's teach our boys to be strong in their feelings. Even the difficult ones. It's OK to talk about their pain so they will learn to tolerate it.

I am not here to affirm my clients. Psychotherapists don't exist to validate you and make you feel good. In fact, quite the contrary; most people leave therapy feeling raw, vulnerable, and emotional. Therapy is hard if you're doing it right. A young adult client recently told me, "I wish you could just agree with me sometimes." We don't treat any other diagnosis this way. Why are we treating gender dysphoria with an affirming-care mindset? Countless transgendered young adults are de-transitioning and screaming to stop transitioning children. They were transitioned too young and changed the way they felt about their gender, many of them worse off because the physical changes are permanent.

The narrative that suicide will inevitably occur if parents do not allow their children to transition is a lie. In fact, suicide is common *after* transitioning genders as well. Many children feel the medical transition was not the answer, and their underlying depression, untreated by the mental health system, takes over. Children's bodies being mutilated before they are developmentally ready to make this decision. I care very deeply for the children who have gender dysphoria. I have treated many of them, and in every case we have gotten to the root of the issue through exploration. I felt so grateful to work alongside such patient, caring, and loving parents who allowed their child to explore their gender identity without rushing into medicalizing it.

KEY TAKEAWAYS

- ▸ Gender identity issues have increased among today's children.
- ▸ Helping a child work through gender dysphoria is the best practice.
- ▸ Gender-affirming care has roots in an industry that stands to profit off increased gender dysphoria diagnoses.

CHAPTER 7

PORNOGRAPHY

*[Porn is] not about equality . . . it's
all about doing something to her.
Not sharing something with her.*[47]
—DON MCPHERSON, AUTHOR
AND FORMER NFL PLAYER

ONLINE PORNOGRAPHY IS STUNTING SEXUAL DEVELOP-
ment and intimacy in this generation of children. The
Internet has given a forum to pornography in a way
that is confusing young people who have not yet formed
their identities. In my practice I notice they begin to get
curious about sex, sexuality, and pornography around
middle school age (ages eleven to fourteen), consistent
with hormone surges and social emotional needs to build
relationships and find a tribe. Many boys at this age are
engaging in online pornography. Parents don't think to talk

to them for various reasons, including naivety about what they could be exposed to online. The pornography experience of these middle schoolers' parents was sneaking their father's *Playboy* magazine and looking at nude photos of women. Many parents think this type of curiosity is normal and that it's OK for children to explore.

At nine, children begin to develop consciousness around individuating to relate to peers and to form interpersonal relationships. It's the beginning of attaching to friends and, eventually, significant others. If they are exposed to online pornography during this critical period in their lives, they risk impeding their learning of how to relate to others outside of their family of origin. This is the low end of risk from exposure. On the higher end of risk, and what I often see in my practice, is sexual development dysfunction. The online pornography of today is not your father's *Playboy*. It's abusive, degrading, and at times traumatizing to watch, and it's not real. Sometimes these are paid actors, and sometimes they are not. The dark world of pornography exploits female actors who have sexual abuse histories and come from low-income households. They are promised a career in adult film but don't get paid what they were told, leaving them feeling trapped in a world that takes advantage of them.

Many children who are exposed to pornography without having talked to their parents develop the notion that this is what sex is, so they try to act that out in real life with one another. This makes them feel regret and remorse afterward because it doesn't fill them up like real intimacy does. Pornography is highly addictive because it feels good without having to deal with the messiness of real-life human relationships. It's a fantasy world. Not knowing how to be intimate, many teens become serial daters and use the term "body" to describe the number of people they have had sex with. They ask one another how many "bodies" they have had, indicating that people are merely physical, nothing else. This feels less intimidating; if you keep it casual, you aren't required to work with a significant other to navigate the conflicts and compromise that come with a relationship.

Teen girls and young adult women have reported to me that they feel lines of consent have been blurred. They agree to sex acts the boys ask them to do from the pornographic videos they watch, and they end up feeling violated. The girls are being asked to do things that are beyond their comfort zone. Girls are especially vulnerable to violent sexual experiences and even rape. Author Nancy Jo Sales interviewed thousands of girls about how the Internet was affecting them. She found that the language being used among teens to describe sex is forceful.[48] Teenagers I have seen for therapy over the years have reported to me that they use such words as "pounded" and "nailed" when talking about sex. The boys are getting a false sense of reality around sex, and the girls are resigned to doing things that make them uncomfortable because they feel they must accept the way that things are.

Many parents are not aware of how pornography has grabbed the attention of their children. Kids and teens, given unfettered access to the Internet, often get curious. Sometimes an innocent Google search will bring up sexual images, and down the rabbit hole they go. Teens report to me that they have even viewed pornography websites during school, both on school-issued devices as well as their own devices! Consider these additional sobering facts:

+ Children as young as seven have been exposed to online pornography.
+ More than half of eleven- to thirteen-year-old have encountered pornography.
+ Of those, only 18 percent sought out porn intentionally. This means that 82 percent came across online pornography unintentionally.
+ Parents are not aware of just how much access their children have; 75 percent of parents claimed their children had not viewed porn, but 53 percent of the children of those parents told the researchers they had viewed porn.[49]

Pornhub, a very popular pornography site with forty-seven billion site visits per year, has been exposed for allowing rape and child sexual abuse content to run rampant on the site. Laila Mickelwait, in her book *Takedown*, details the horrific ways in which victims are being re-traumatized by the knowledge that video recordings of their attacks are on the site for all to see. The videos were being monetized with ads that offered pay to download content. Laila has been working tirelessly to get this site shut down. As of the writing of this book, she has made massive progress, but there are still legal battles in process as the victims are suing Pornhub. Pornhub was a crime scene for many years, and it has been a years-long battle to take down this giant.[50]

Parents, talk to your kids about sex long before they are exposed to pornography. I have heard from many parents that they don't talk to their children about sex because they think health class in school suffices. Talking about sex with children starts early and often. It begins with naming the correct medical names for their private body parts. Many parents come up with cute names to avoid the discomfort of talking about it. Children should see their parents giving each other physical affection in the form of hand-holding, hugging, cuddling, and kissing. This allows them to be comfortable seeing healthy intimacy. Let your kids know you are comfortable talking about sex, sexuality, and intimacy. If they feel you are squeamish, they will be too.

Foster a culture in which no subject is off-limits. If they don't talk to you, they will go to their friends and/or the Internet. You want them to get the information from you, not a Google search. Talk to them about pornography. They need to hear it from you. You want to be the one to influence them, to impart your wisdom and values before someone else does. Encourage them to have real-life interactions with significant others, to go on dates, learn how to communicate effectively, and master conflict resolution. We have a generation of children who are not learning how to relate to one another. They are increasingly lonely and isolated and may never have long-lasting intimate relationships as a result. Yes, these conversations are uncomfortable. Your kids will hate this talk! They will squirm, roll their eyes, and tell you to stop. Too bad. You must educate yourself and talk to them. They need you.

My son was around eleven when I went to my husband and told him it was time to have the pornography talk. He sighed and reluctantly agreed. Being the husband of a therapist, he knew he wasn't going to get out of this discomfort. I said, "OK, so here's how it going to go: We are going to tell him pornography isn't real, these are actors, and sex is between two people who love each other and it's beautiful." My husband said, "Wait, stop right there. We are *not* going to tell an eleven-year-old boy that sex is beautiful. I will do the talking." I agreed and was happy to oblige! As predicted, our son was squirmy and not happy to be talking about pornography with us. But this talk was necessary. We talked about relationships and intimacy and the importance of experiencing real-life human interaction. We continue to model a healthy relationship with communication and physical affection. Children need us to show them the way.

KEY TAKEAWAYS

▸ Children have unprecedented access to online pornography and have likely seen it without your knowledge.

▸ Use of online pornography is affecting the development of sexuality and reducing intimacy.

▸ Parents need to gain knowledge of the dangers and ways in which children are exposed.

▸ Parents, push past the discomfort and talk to your children and adolescents about sex and pornography.

CHAPTER 8

CONNECTION TO SELF

Receive the children in reverence,
educate them in love, and send
them forth in freedom.[51]
—RUDOLPH STEINER

THE CONNECTION TO SELF IS THE LAST PHASE IN THE four parts of the child development wheel. It's all connected. Children's bodies, brains, and emotional and spiritual development happen in unison, symbiotic of one another. You can't have one without the others. According to Rudolf Steiner, an educator and child development expert, "The human being is a threefold being of spirit, soul, and body whose capacities unfold in three developmental stages on the path to adulthood: early childhood, middle childhood, and adolescence."[52] Steiner's stages of development happen every seven years, 0–7, 7–14, and

14–21. Two years into those seven-year phases, major developmental milestones occur around independence.

At each of the two-year phases (two, nine, and sixteen), individuation occurs. Each time a child individuates and is supported in it, they develop a connection to themselves. They emerge as an individual and separate from their parents or caregivers. This is natural and healthy. If they are grounded in their sense of self, they can develop critical thinking skills and discernment. The two-year-old finds the word "no," the nine-year-old questions the existence of Santa Claus and the tooth fairy, and the sixteen-year-old begins to think about his future.

Unfortunately, there is so much disruption to the individuating process due to technology. Children don't even have to think for themselves anymore. If you can't enable your critical thought process, self-awareness and your connection to self is broken. It's called *attunement*—the ability to connect with yourself, thus being able to connect to others. Consider the weather app on smart devices as an example of something most people think of as benign but is hindering children's critical thinking skills. The weather is our favorite form of small talk. Everyone likes to talk about it, and it affects us all. There is often discussion about what the weather will be tomorrow or next week, and many people have become accustomed to looking on their smart devices for the answer.

This is fine for us adults who grew up with the ability to use our minds and figure out how to go about the day without knowing what the weather is going to be. We might pack a raincoat or umbrella if it looks cloudy in the morning, because perhaps it is going to rain later (or, for those of us in colder states, to pack a hat and gloves in case it is freezing or snowy). I remember opening the door in the morning to see how it felt outside before deciding what to wear and how to go about my day. Today's children tap a screen, and immediately the weather is at their fingertips. They will know all day what the weather will be, and if it's going to rain or snow, they will know what is preventing them from using necessary skills for life. You can think of it like math; my son often talks about how he's never going to use math in his life. My answer is that may be true, but math teaches life skills that you're going to need forever. It's teaching you how to work through your frustration, how to use your analytical skills. It's a way for your brain to practice, because you need those skills for life whether you have a job that requires math or not.

The weather app is the David compared to the Goliath that is artificial intelligence (AI). Individual apps are what I consider a slippery slope, desensitizing us to encouraging our children to think for themselves. Children are using AI to solve their problems for them. ChatGPT can write a paper for you in thirty seconds flat. You can even tell it to write at your grade level, so your teacher is none the wiser. Thankfully, most teachers are well versed in recognizing this type of cheating, but modalities are only going to get more sophisticated. Students can scan a math problem and solve it immediately, including the "show your work" steps behind how they got the answer. New features on smart devices allow you to take a picture of an event and it will automatically add it to your calendar.

Also, how common is it to recognize a face but not a name? Smart devices can now search your phone for details surrounding meeting someone and recall their name for you. You can ask Siri to text people on their birthdays, an act that shows you are thinking of someone you love and recognizing them. My mom instilled in us to remember birthdays and to personally reach out. She still even strategically mails birthday cards so they arrive on the day of your birthday. When we allow children to use these features, we are taking away their ability to connect. The human side of us is fractured for convenience. This is teaching children that perfection is the goal when you use a device to think for you so you don't forget someone's birthday.

But programmed perfectionism is a mistake. Forgetting a birthday is something that makes us human. Children should learn that if you make a mistake, you are responsible for fixing it. There is a lesson in apologizing and communicating to the person that your relationship is important to you. That's what helps us connect to other people. Experiencing the painful feelings of forgetting someone you love is important. Connecting to your feelings is the first part of connecting to yourself, then others.

Furthermore, many families have AI devices central to the home, commanding it to play a song, look something up, and get instant gratification for what you asked. Adults may find these innovations convenient and many businesses are using AI to enhance their operations and practices. But this isn't about the adults. We must think of how it is affecting the children. Adults, you have developed naturally, allowed to explore your critical thinking capabilities and formulate your own thoughts. Children are now commanding a device to do things for them that they should be doing themselves, stripping them of the ability to develop patience and wait for what they want. Alexa has given children the opportunity to not have to lift a finger. AI doesn't have feelings. You can speak to it any way you want. Empathy is not even a factor. It's like their own personal robot.

What's next, Apple Vision Pro goggles that deprive you of your senses? How long will it be until it's the norm to see children wearing AI goggles everywhere? Your eyes literally control the apps on your device. This reminds me of a child I encountered while on vacation in northern Michigan. If you have ever been to this part of the world, you know the sights are beautiful. Water as far as the eye can see. We were at a lookout point and there was one of those telescopes you put a quarter in. A boy asked my husband and me if we had a quarter and we didn't, so his sister said, "You don't need the telescope, you can use your EYES." She emphasized the word eyes. His response? He pulled his iPhone out of his pocket and said, "I'll use my iPhone." He emphasized the "I" in iPhone, replacing his sister's suggestion to use his actual eye to look. I implore you to think about all devices, apps, and tools that take away a child's ability to think for themselves.

These are critical periods of development that should not be tampered with.

Individuate at 2

The process of separation happens over time, and at two the child is ready to begin individuating. Obviously, two-year-olds cannot take care of themselves, but through their behavior they are saying, "I want to do it eventually." An example of this is the child who climbs out of their crib, a common two-year-old's practice. The child is telling their parents they are ready for a bed. It's a subconscious form of communication. A bed without bars means freedom to get up and out when they want. This is always a challenging time for parents, as newfound freedom comes with constantly getting up and out until the novelty wears off. This behavior is healthy and right on schedule. Follow their lead; they know what they need. My niece knew she was ready to potty train by retrieving some underwear that was waiting for the right time. She knew before my sister did that she was ready. My sister allowed her to try, and she was successful. Only two accidents and she was fully fledged.

Closet confession: I am a parent who gets sad when my kids separate. I'm often in denial about it even though I know that it is coming and when. Someone else usually must point it out, my husband or my mom, and then when they do, I have a grieving period before I let go. It is the hardest part of parenting for me. And it's a family joke that my daughter has benefited from the mistakes we made with her older brother, Oliver. I did much better to allow her to separate than I did him. Despite my best efforts to protect him from growing up, his strong mind was very clever, which became apparent on an occasion when my brother tried to sit in Oliver's special chair that had his name on it. I became uncomfortable as Oliver grew agitated, and my brother asked him, "Why can't I sit in your chair?" Oliver thought about it very intently and responded, "You should sit on the couch, you will be more comfortable." My brother thought this answer was too good not to get out of the chair! An adult sits on the couch, a two-year-old sits in the chair with his name on it, and all is right with the world.

If you have older kids, you probably remember when they were around two years of age they would say, "Do it by myself." Children at this age have a mind of their own. When my nephew was two, he demonstrated this well. He was at his grandmother's house and began playing with fine china. His grandmother told him no, obviously not wanting him to break her valuables. He responded with "Bye!" She asked, "Where are you going." He said, "Taita's house!" Taita is my mom. He was telling her that his other grandmother would allow him to do what he wants, which is not true—my mom wouldn't allow that either, but in his mind, he was not going to be told what to do.

If you are a new parent, be sure to let your children do things by themselves, within reason, of course, and considering safety. Many children at this age want to learn independent tasks such as cooking. This is a great time to get a stepstool and place it right next to you in the kitchen. They can pour, measure, and mix. Praising them for their efforts will surely go a long way and reinforce that learning new tasks is encouraged. This fosters connection to themselves if they can express and communicate something they want, then they find peace in knowing that they can do so in the world later. It might seem like the simple act of asking for independence is so small. I assure you it is not. It is the beginning of perseverance and determination. These qualities are foundational, the building blocks of being able to stand in yourself all throughout your life to ground yourself and knowing that you have the answer, you have the power, you can solve your own problems. This has never been more important than it is for the iGeneration because of all they must contend with.

Nine-year change

A period in development referred to as middle childhood occurs from the ages of nine to twelve. Many parents notice that their children who were mild mannered before middle childhood suddenly become emotional, start resisting rules, and challenge boundaries right around the age of nine. Children go through an exceptionally large growth spurt, and this time can be confusing both for parents and children. While children are changing, parents do not understand what is happening and may not know how to react. Middle childhood is a unique time in a child's life. It should be understood by parents and adults who work with children. This is a time for separation. In the early

1900s Steiner dubbed it "the nine-year change." Children see themselves as individuals outside of the family. Prior to nine, the family is the center of a child's world. After nine (some kids show signs of this at eight or eight and a half), they begin to become interested in separating from their parents. They develop a consciousness around worldly experiences they never had before. You may notice that friends become more important at this age, and with that comes the need to make and keep friends, as well as fit in. This emotional process comes with some anxiety because, while it is exciting to see yourself as an independent being, it can be jarring, and children can begin to have fears and worries that previously were not in their consciousness.

Children at this age have one foot in early childhood and one foot in adolescence. Being somewhere in the middle can mean they do not know how to ground themselves. Therefore, they become emotional. Parents may see emotional outbursts over what seems like nothing, along with regression in autonomous tasks (maybe they were doing something independently and suddenly ask for help). Parents are often bewildered at how their "sweet," mild-mannered child is suddenly having outbursts. With the emotional growth of feeling ready to separate comes some trepidation. It's scary to separate from parents, and there is often some reverting back to early childhood. For example, you may see stuffed animals come back if they stopped playing with them as they grew. This is all very normal and part of the process of transitioning into middle childhood. Parents can support their children during this time by allowing them the freedom to experience their anxious feelings. There is no need for therapy. I get a lot of calls about nine- and ten-year-olds because many parents feel worried about their children. Anxiety in this stage is normal. Parents need to allow for their own discomfort so their child can move through theirs; remember, you are the container.

Also, the feeling of fear materializes during the nine-year change. My daughter was eight, almost nine when I noticed her nine-year change. We have a public pool nearby that has a high dive. When she was five, she climbed those steps, walked right up to the end of the diving board, and bravely jumped without hesitation— and then continuously went back for more. She did this every summer . . . until she was eight. Suddenly she was scared and wouldn't even attempt to climb the steps to the diving board. The conscious becomes more sophisticated, and children begin to think of scenarios where something could go wrong. That same summer she froze on stage during her dance recital, forgetting some steps. Being on stage was something she had done since she was four. She had always been very comfortable. She was aware of the audience, and it felt intimidating to her. I made sure to talk to her about the way it felt to be scared and that it was normal at her age. I encouraged her to work through the fear, and by the next summer she was back to jumping off the high dive and being comfortable on stage.

The nine-year changes also come with some teenage behavior. Out of a desire for more independence, kids push back on rules during this time. They will likely question the rules and want to know why things are the way they are. Kids at this age develop a deeper consciousness and can understand abstract thinking, so they become more sophisticated in conversations. They are literally in the middle of their childhoods. You can imagine how confusing that must be for children and parents if they don't know what is going on.

In boys, this change looks a bit different than it does in girls. As we have discussed, boys internalize their feelings because they think expressing them shows weakness. They aren't told that there is strength in vulnerability. They also don't know what is going on emotionally. Kids don't have the vocabulary for their feelings. They literally don't have the words to communicate what is inside. Today's boys aren't getting what they need developmentally early on so by age nine, they aren't experiencing the desire to separate or have independence, and they don't know how to communicate their needs. They aren't even aware of what is missing.

Girls are better at this. They display outbursts of emotion, and in that way they are telling their parents something. Parents are forced to pay attention. In the years before I stopped seeing children, I received a lot of calls for ten-year-old girls because of the big bursts of emotion that come during this time. I once had a mom in my office crying with relief after I explained the nine-year change as the reason she was seeing such emotionality so suddenly in her daughter. She truly thought something was wrong, but I reassured her it was completely normal. There is no need for therapy during this time. It's perfectly normal and necessary for children to go through this phase, with all the feelings that come from it. I'll never forget when that sweet little girl said, "So when I'm eleven, it will go away?"

Boys don't have this same emotionality. Today's boys display this phase of development much differently. The way it manifests makes them appear helpless. They don't complete activities of daily living, such as picking up their socks, brushing their teeth, and being ready to go somewhere on time. Their executive-functioning skills don't develop well. It looks the opposite of what it should be. Though it looks like they aren't ready for independence, it's more that many boys at this age today don't *want* the independence that comes with middle childhood. They don't feel sure enough of themselves to separate. They revert to toddler-like behaviors, wanting developmental tasks to be done for them. Many parents continue to take care of their boys' tasks that should be done on their own during this time because their boys don't seem capable. I see many fathers step in with discipline, only to be thwarted by mothers who think their sons still need help and reminders to pick up their socks. Parents often want to impart consequences on behavior and lack of responsibility, but today's culture of parenting sees this as a punishment and doesn't want boys to feel the discomfort that goes along with accountability. Many parents are not following their instincts because they are following the norm.

Parents often don't recognize the need to allow their children independence during middle childhood. They see their children as too young and not ready. I had the honor of meeting Lenore Skenazy, who wrote an article about allowing her nine-year-old boy to find his way home from a department store in New York City using the subway *by himself*. He had asked for independence and wanted to accomplish that task on his own. She allowed it, wrote about it, and within days she was all over the media being called America's worst mother. She went on to write a book called *Free-Range Kids* and started a movement called Let Grow to advocate for childhood independence.[53] I remember reading her article when my son was just a baby. I loved how she defended her choice because it was in her son's best interest.

This was an important milestone for Lenore and her son. He needed her to trust him and his ability to separate in a healthy way. She didn't know about the nine-year change but instinctively knew it was what he needed. She used her attunement and connection with him to give him what he needed developmentally. When we met, I told her that he was right on schedule with wanting that independence because of the nine-year change, and she was interested in that information as it put the pieces together. However, she didn't need to know the developmental piece at the time because she used her motherly instincts. We are so far out of balance in our culture today; parents are overwhelmed, busy, and distracted, and this has taken away our ability to use our God-given instincts to know what our children need!

Today's children and teens don't trust themselves to navigate the uncertain because they didn't get the independence at nine to figure this out and work through their anxiety. They don't know they can get through hard things. They don't feel strong or sure of themselves. They don't know they can experience pain and discomfort and get to the other side. They avoid pain and discomfort. Their development has been fractured.

As a mother and a child psychotherapist, I've noticed that today's children can be separated into two groups. One group's schedules are full of adult-run, organized activities. The other group's kids have no interests, motivation, or ability to push themselves out of their comfort zone, and they end up using too much digital technology. Having a balance between the two groups seems out of reach. There are no longer children playing independently and being given freedom to explore the world away from their parents' homes. The real magic of childhood happens when there is unorganized, unstructured free play, with kids of all ages working together without adult interruption. There is so much learning that happens when children are free. They motivate one another, challenge one another, confront one another, and learn how to resolve conflict.

Our culture doesn't allow for this type of freedom, and children struggle if they're not getting what they need during this time in their development. I have seen many ten-year-olds in my practice who become frustrated with the lack of independence. They often project that on to their parents because parents are emotionally safe. Kids' feelings will come out with you because they know you are not going anywhere. I had a ten-year-old girl come in because her parents were experiencing her as angry and resistant. Her mom and dad were perplexed, as they felt they were giving her a proper balance of organized activities she enjoyed and free time. There was no prior conflict, and the family was intact. I worked with her parents to understand that she was looking for opportunities to be brave and have experiences with friends separate from her parents. They worked on ways in which she could be a leader in her friend group and organize meetups at the park or bike rides in the neighborhood. She began to fill herself up in the way she needed and no longer projected her frustration at her parents.

I will never forget one of the things I learned in my child development class while I was getting my bachelor's in psychology: Kindergarteners in Japan are encouraged to work through their conflicts on their own in school. I remember seeing videos of teachers waiting nearby while children argued. The adults never intervened; the children figured it out. The lesson? Those children gained lifelong skills. That is what children in schools should be learning today. So many young people don't know how to communicate because their entire lives are either structured and supervised by adults or isolated from social interaction with peers. Mixed-age classrooms can offer so much value to children—older kids mentoring the younger kids, the younger kids looking up to them and accepting lessons more so than from their own parents. The older kids develop self-esteem because they feel like successful leaders. The richness of these experiences lies in children figuring out how to navigate social interaction and learning from one another, not being told what to do but discovering it on their own.

Thinking about this, I was reminded that today's children are being stunted when it comes to learning from mixed ages. My daughter was involved in a recent community theater production. The age range was eight to fourteen. At a parent meeting before the auditions, it took over an hour to go through everything the theater staff had already sent in an email. There was no reason to have a meeting. In the meeting there was a lot of pressure to sign up to help with rehearsals. I was baffled by this because there were at least four adults employed by the theater to put on productions. I wasn't sure why they needed so much help from parents. I learned the reason when I picked my daughter up from rehearsal the first day.

The dismissal policy was that parents were to come into the building, check in with a parent volunteer, provide their child's name, and wait for the children to come out. This, they said, was due to safety concerns. The organizers didn't think the kids could cross the street on their own to get to their parents' cars. The theater is in an extremely safe neighborhood with traffic lights and pedestrian signals. The building is very small, and there were at least fifty kids being dismissed at once. It was total chaos. There is no reason they needed a parent volunteer because children, especially at these ages, need independence. It would've been perfectly fine for them to leave the building on their own and find their parents on the street. The older kids could help the younger kids. This would give them some responsibility and help them to feel capable. The younger kids would benefit from this modeling. What a pity for them not to have had that opportunity.

You may remember a time when kids played together outside, roaming freely around the neighborhood with no adult supervision. When I was growing up, my neighborhood was filled with kids. We were outside playing every day, even in the cold winter months, and if we weren't playing outside, we were back-and-forth to one another's houses. Parents were involved minimally as they were just there to check on and feed us. My Lebanese mother had (and still has) the favorite house to be because there was always a lot of food.

During middle childhood my son was becoming more independent in his desire to be in the neighborhood on his own with friends, but he wasn't sure of himself, and I was confused as to why he lacked self-confidence. I was also confused at why he wasn't doing tasks independently even though we had been teaching and encouraging them. I understood the nine-year change and thought I was giving him what he needed. Middle childhood is at the end of the social emotional phase of development, when children need to be building their confidence. Our culture has adopted the thinking that building children's confidence comes from the "everybody wins" mentality. But handing out participation trophies and making children happy all the time are *not* how they gain confidence. This way of thinking is particularly damaging for boys because of their propensity for competition. It's quite the opposite. Boys need to feel competent. They need to work through a frustrating task and come out the other side feeling proud and capable. The reward is their pride in themselves.

A ten-year-old boy I once worked with—I will call him Tom—was experiencing conflict with his parents because he wasn't always doing his homework, and if he did do it, he wasn't turning it in. As we explored reasons why, it came out that other boys in his class were doing the same. Tom felt that there was no point for him to complete his work if others weren't. There were no consequences from the teacher either. Just a simple, "Get it to me when you can." I asked Tom about the girls, and he revealed that they were conscientious and on top of their responsibilities. I wondered why he wasn't comparing himself to them. He was clear that it was the boys he compared himself to and if there was no competition to be a good student compared to his male peers, he wasn't interested. The competition is what makes boys want to try. The bonus is the trophy, but only for those who worked for it. That's how boys become confident. It's crucial they are allowed the separation and independence the nine-year change brings. If they do, it locks in their confidence, which should be developed by twelve.

Parents, you can foster independence during this time by allowing your nine-year-olds to do more for themselves. They can also serve the family by mowing the lawn, walking the family dog, and learning how to prepare a meal. If it's available, they can walk or ride their bike to run an errand. This will build their confidence and allow them to choose independence more often. This frees parents up from the cliché of being the "nag."

Sixteen and driving

A time for a final surge of independence before teenagers leave home, turning sixteen is a rite of passage. A teenager's brain is now more ready to individuate and experience a life separate from their parents. But they are not fully ready to leave home, with one foot in and one foot out.

Why are teenagers not getting their driver's licenses?

This section is for the family that has the means to obtain a driver's license. Many teens and their families are not able to pay for driver's training, a car, car insurance, and gas, so driving is unattainable. If you are one of those families, driving isn't the only way to foster independence. This can be done in any way that works for your family. For example, navigating public transit independently is a means for teenagers to gain a sense of self-reliance.

In recent years, a lack of motivation and urgency to obtain driver's licenses have become increasingly common among teens, which is a puzzling trend for many of us older individuals. As someone who vividly remembers the excitement of turning sixteen and getting my license, it's disheartening to witness this change. I could not wait to make it official, secure my license, and drive off into the sunset independently—I didn't even care that it was in my mother's minivan!

One significant reason for the decline in teen drivers is the rise of automation and convenient online services. In today's tech-driven world, it's easier than ever to order anything we need from the comfort of our homes. From an emotional standpoint, this fosters social anxiety in teens as they have become accustomed to staying home and avoiding crowded places or traffic. The 2020 lock-downs further solidified this behavior for these "screen-agers," exacerbating their declining desire to drive.

Additionally, parents play a crucial role in their children's decision to get a license. Many parents experience increasing anxiety as their children approach driving age. This represents a huge loss of control for parents, as they must trust their children while simultaneously letting go of their fears about other drivers on the road. This projected anxiety can negatively influence teenagers' perception of driving and their own capabilities. If a parent doesn't trust their teenager to drive, they are sending the teen-ager a message that they aren't capable. The lack of trust from the parent fractures self-trust, a necessary trait for growing teenagers.

Moreover, a lack of self-trust and agency, largely influenced by technology, is contributing to the decline in teen drivers. The iGeneration is growing up in a world where external rewards are readily available for almost everything they do. They are extrinsically rewarded for answering a question right in school, attending an after-school activity, and doing household chores at home. Instead of an external reward, they need an *internal* reward for working hard in school, doing extracurricular activities, and at home, pushing through their frustration and desire to quit and coming out the other end feeling good about accomplishing difficult tasks. This overreliance on extrinsic rewards hinders the development of intrinsic motivation and the ability to work through challenging situations.

Many teenagers don't trust themselves and are anxious of uncertain situations because of a lack of ability to complete challenging tasks early in their development. After exploring this with my teenage clients, I have determined that all along the way their parents prevented them from doing things on their own. As a result, they aren't able to work through frustration, fear, or painful feelings. To do something grown-up such as drive, for example, they can't overcome feelings of anxiety. It's called "learned helplessness"—a taught behavior, not always intentional, but nonetheless something that parents need to be aware of. Working with parents can help them learn how to be uncomfortable with their children's growth.

For parents who struggle to allow their teenagers to drive because of their own fears, driving isn't just about being scared to allow your fifteen-year-old to take driver's training. It's the culmination of years of enabling your children to not complete the tasks of development. It's defining them as not capable or ready. It's continuing to enable them by driving them around after they are sixteen. At some point, and it's never too late, you must let go and surrender your feelings of fear. Those feelings about your child not being capable are really about *you* not feeling adequate. Remember the mirror: You look at them and their lack of growing up, and you subconsciously blame yourself. You can push through that, face it, and let it move through you. Their independence depends on it.

> You might lose your body out there in the world, but if you stay here, you lose your soul.
> —*Jordan Peterson*

Another thing to consider is that it is dangerous out in the world, but it's more dangerous for your older children to stay with you, safe and protected at home. Not going out in the world and experiencing life will prevent them from fully launching, and those consequences are greater. So many parents, even after allowing their teenagers to drive, can't fully let go. They use tracking apps such as Life360 to keep tabs on them. Life360 allows parents to monitor their teens' speed, location, and even the volume on the radio. Touted as necessary for safety, these apps bring anxious parents' comfort. Yes, it's a compromise for a parent who is afraid to allow their teenager to drive and giving them the freedom to do so. However, the use of these apps doesn't give the teen full independence and still sends the message that they cannot be trusted. Teenagers sixteen and over should not be tracked; they should be trusted. If you are a parent who doesn't feel your child can be trusted, then you have some work to do. Your two-year-old should be trusted to know when she is full and finished eating, your nine-year-old should be trusted to get to a friend's house on his own or walk to the store and buy some milk, and your sixteen-year-old should have learned how to be a safe driver after taking driver's training and practicing with a permit. These are the independent tasks of childhood that are to be done at the appropriate ages so that when they are fully grown and on their own, they will be ready to thrive in the world.

Apps for convenience have taken over our lives. If we aren't careful, they will erode (or maybe already have) our critical thinking and decision-making skills. Think about the navigation apps such as Google Maps. If a teen relies on the app to tell them how to get from point A to point B, they won't learn the roads and will never experience getting lost. And that's an important part of learning how to drive: relying on your own navigation skills to find the way, reading maps, figuring out which directions certain roads go. Technology is not a sure thing. You can't rely on it. You can rely on yourself. There is no better lesson for a driving teenager.

Since 2010, there has been a 139 percent increase in anxiety in US undergrads.[54] With each phase of individuation, it's the parents' role to step back. Of course, just a little step at age two, more of one at age nine, and a very large one at age sixteen. What I mean by step back is that *you are the boundary*. You set the rules and give consequences when they are not followed. You also allow for natural consequences when necessary. Don't rescue them. If your middle schooler or high schooler forgets their lunch, let them figure out what to do. Don't solve the problem by bringing their lunch or sending them money. If they get a bad grade or feel their teacher was unfair to them, don't email the teacher or call the principal. Allow them to talk to the teacher, find a solution, learn to communicate. This builds your connection with your child because you are giving them what they need. You are the template for how they build a connection with themselves. By accepting the ways they separate in each developmental stage, you are allowing them to have a deeper connection with themselves and a growing ability to trust themselves to solve their own problems. That's the path to independence.

KEY TAKEAWAYS

- ▸ Individuation in childhood leads to a connection to self, the last phase of The Four Parts of Child Development.
- ▸ It's important that children have boundaries around technology during times of individuation so they can learn how to think for themselves, a necessary component to a connection to self.
- ▸ This is a time for separation; it's natural, healthy, and necessary.
- ▸ Parents can support independence in age-appropriate ways to foster growth.

Call to Action

If you haven't already, be sure to download the *Free to Fly Kit* by going to the website https://nicole-runyon. mykajabi.com/-bonus-material or scanning the QR code below.

There you will find a hidden bonus to help you with the chapter you just read. Simply enter your name and email to receive the kit. Then find the *Activities Cheat Sheet*. This is a robust list of age-appropriate activities your child can do independently and ones you can do together, including chores.

CHAPTER 9

ALLOWING FOR DISCOMFORT

*Children are great imitators. So give
them something great to imitate.*
—ANONYMOUS

Do you have an emotional issue that keeps surfacing? One that you thought you were done with long ago? I do—boundaries!

I really struggle with boundaries. I tell myself it's because I grew up in a big family. Nothing was sacred. I didn't have space to myself, so I don't know how to give myself what I need. However, the more I think about it, the more I realize this issue is embedded deep in my soul, an ancestral wound, because it keeps showing up. Ancestral wounds are passed down generationally because the one before does not resolve them. Generationally, we have developed maladaptive ways of managing pain and we don't model healthy practices for our children. Children mimic their parents, and it usually takes a self-aware generation to end the pain that is continuously passed down. Despite my best efforts at "coping skill" this family curse away, I have come to realize it is what I am here to learn so I don't pass it on to the next generation.

My boundary issue has manifested in my parenting at times, and with every "no" I tell my children, I feel healing. Healing doesn't mean something feels good. It often feels wretched. Parents, we need to hold the space for our own discomfort to allow our children to be uncomfortable. Saying no and having boundaries are healing. Children are supposed to learn how to set their own boundaries and how to respect their parents' boundaries in the developmental stage from eighteen months to three years. Yes, that early! As discussed, this is the "will and authority" stage of psychosocial development—the terrible twos, or the "no" stage. It's a time when they are learning how to stand in their will; that's why the word "no" is so prevalent and why this time has been dubbed the terrible twos. It's *supposed* to be hard for parents. It's a dance for the parent/child relationship for the parent to respect their child's "no" and for a child to respect their parents' "no."

I hear many parents say they find it's not the terrible twos that are the worst, it's age three that is the hardest. That's because the will and authority stage often do not go well in today's parenting culture. Many parents are afraid to exert their authority during this stage of development so children do not learn good boundaries, and the balance is off. Today's parents often allow their two-year-old to have too much authority because they are afraid to say no. Then at three, when children are supposed to be learning how to be autonomous, they have a difficult time doing independent tasks on their own. Parents react to this by doing too much for their children, and they don't learn how to trust themselves or feel agency. This leads to more meltdowns and tantrums in this phase of development.

Boundaries are important and necessary, and if they are as uncomfortable for you as they are for me, I feel your pain. What parents of this generation need to know is that it is OK to make your kids uncomfortable. It's necessary, it's a sacrifice, and it will be hard for you, but it's to their benefit. Just know that you must be willing to do the hard things so your children can go through natural developmental processes. It will be worth it. Not just for your children, but for generations to come.

I am a boy mom. My son and I have a close connection, and we are now in a phase of life where I don't tuck him in at night because I go to bed before him! He's fifteen and becoming a man. At the same time, he respects that I am still his mother and am still in charge! I've learned over the years he needs strong boundaries so that he feels supported and protected in his growth. His height of six feet to my five feet is kind of hilarious, and he loves to show me that he is physically stronger and bigger by picking me up like a baby when I least expect it. Sometimes I yell at him to put me down, and then I laugh so hard I can't even speak. I remind myself that this is his way of playfully exerting his power. He wants to show me he is physically stronger, not because he wants to hurt me but because it makes him feel good about himself. That's what boys need in order to feel confident. They need to know they can physically dominate when it is necessary for their protection. It's the basis for their psychology.

Things are good between us now, but it wasn't always this way. His middle childhood was rough. The secret sauce for a boy is in building his confidence early and allowing him to be independent when he is ready by middle childhood. It didn't help that my son's middle childhood was during the lockdowns of 2020, and he wasn't getting the social interaction he desperately needed. I had so much motherly guilt that I wasn't enough for him. He was struggling, and I blamed myself and couldn't see outside of that to help him. My son's middle childhood went awry because I had it all wrong, and a video recording of him when he was just a year old helped me see that.

My husband was recording us playing. We were dancing and listening to music. Lots of fun, laughs, and giggles. Then our son crawled over to a low-height bed and began climbing onto it. He was grunting and struggling to get up. I let him struggle for a moment and then I did what many mothers do: I helped him up on the bed! He could have done it on his own, he was almost there, but recognizing his discomfort, I couldn't bear it, so I helped him.

As I rewatched this interaction, it hit me like a train. I did not allow him to be uncomfortable and work through his frustration. He was not distressed; he was simply frustrated at the task, and I should have let him do it on his own. This is what creates independence. This is what builds self-confidence, autonomy, and self-trust. It's no wonder his middle childhood wasn't going well. That was one recording of me not allowing his independence (such a gift for us parents today to have our mistakes recorded), and I started thinking about how many other times I had done this throughout his childhood without even knowing it. Though I understood what he needed in middle childhood and gave him some independence, his confidence wasn't built, so he wasn't able to have it. Confidence building starting at younger ages scaffolds the child to be ready for independence at nine.

What we were experiencing with our son in middle childhood was a direct result of all those times I helped him with a developmental task that he should have worked through on his own. He didn't want to learn to tie his shoes because I waited until he was five to teach him, all the while doing it for him. This was from good intentions. I thought I was taking care of him, and his sister wasn't born until he was five so I was available to him. Children need frustrating developmental tasks early on through each phase of development or they can't learn to trust themselves. Even if you as a parent are available to do it for them, you shouldn't. They need you to model it for them first, then teach them, then be in the background and allow them to try it on their own, and when it's frustrating let them keep trying. Doing hard things in early childhood is the best gift we can give them.

After I watched the recording, I showed it to my husband and said, "This is where I went wrong," quickly following that with, "Why didn't you stop me?" He laughed and said no one was going to stop me! Well, that is true; he had a good point. A father's voice is important, but a mother often adopts the misconception that she must take on the task of child-rearing. I often hear mothers talk about wanting help from their partners, and fathers feeling they don't know how to help because their partners don't like the way they do it. Moms often have a system, and dads take a back seat because they don't know when and how to jump into the family system.

I saw this in me when my second child was born. My husband took on the task of caring for our oldest when he could, and I didn't like the spoon he was using to stir our son's oatmeal! It wasn't the "right" spoon. Even in my postpartum haze, though, I had enough good sense not to say that to him. Instead, I did some self-examination and learned that I was having trouble letting go of what I thought was "my job." My job to care for our son, feed him, and do things for him. The truth was, he needed me to separate from him so his dad could take a more active role in his life. It was good for my husband and my son to connect without me. However, my son was five and he had not gone through the phase of autonomy and independence well because I was doing too much for him. I didn't teach him to wipe after toileting, or brush his teeth without reminders, or allow him to take care of his hygiene on his own.

Big "T" trauma versus small "t" trauma

As mentioned, this book is written for parents of children who have made mistakes, because that's normal, not for the parents of children who have been traumatized. I think the word "trauma" has been overused, much like other mental health vernacular. I want to clear this up for parents, because discerning between trauma and painful human experiences is key to allowing our children discomfort when appropriate. All too often as a society we treat children as though they are not capable of managing hardship. For example, losing a family pet is not traumatic. It's sad. It's painful. But it's not traumatic. Many people bring their children in for therapy to talk about grief and loss immediately when the loss occurs. We must put this in perspective because while loss is painful, it should not be pathologized. I am in no way saying that children should not have therapy for grief and loss, but only if it is warranted. Give it time, because you may find that learning how to tolerate painful feelings allows the child to feel agency and control over the situation. Feelings move through us if we allow them. I would consider this a small "t" trauma, the kind that may not need anything other than time and love from you. If it seems they are avoiding their feelings and it is coming out in their behavior or in other maladaptive ways, then therapy is appropriate to help them move through those feelings.

Big "T" trauma are real threats to a child's safety, such as pervasive physical abuse, sexual abuse of any kind, neglect (physical and emotional), hunger, poverty, and economic uncertainty, as well as growing up with a substance-abusing parent or in a domestic violence situation. Any of these is considered trauma that would require therapy and a healing process with many coping skills and support. All these describe what we call ACEs (adverse childhood events). They can lead to mental health issues, fractures in brain development, and chronic health conditions in children who experience multiple ACEs throughout their childhoods. These children should be treated for their trauma in a therapeutic setting with a trained professional who can help them move through their trauma and find a place of feeling in control of themselves, with the power to move forward.

I would argue that in cases where there is no trauma, many kids are acting out as if there has been. Small "t" trauma can occur when children are not allowed natural child developmental processes because their parents are doing tasks of development for them. Many kids today are subconsciously angry with their parents for not giving them what they need, so they act out. Parents, you must dig deep into yourselves. When your child is exhibiting concerning behavior and emotions, ask yourself where this might be coming from. Find out what's behind the behavior.

I see many kids who experience this wound and exhibit bad behavior in the form of entitlement. In these cases, the child who doesn't take responsibility for himself is punishing his parents for not doing enough for him. Parents overcompensate and fall all over themselves trying to solve the problem. This makes it worse. They are creating monsters. By making things too easy for kids, they don't allow them to take ownership over themselves. The kids have no self-control, so they place inappropriate demands on their parents. This makes them look weak, ill, disordered, and dysfunctional as their parents continue to take care of them and don't push them out of their comfort zone.

Things have been made easier and more comfortable for children since the millennials (born between 1980–1997) emerged. Generations of children growing up with a high level of comfort has prevented them from tolerating negative feelings. Suicide among young people is on the rise. By 2015, suicide rates had risen 33 percent, an all-time high in thirty years.[55] According to Jean Twenge in her article "Have Smartphones Destroyed a Generation?," "Girls have also borne the brunt of the rise in depressive symptoms among today's teens. Boys' depressive symptoms increased by 21 percent from 2012 to 2015, while girls' increased by 50 percent—more than twice as much. The rise in suicide, too, is more pronounced among girls. Although the rate increased for both sexes, three times as many 12- to 14-year-old girls killed themselves in 2015 as in 2007, compared with twice as many boys."[56] After the lockdowns of 2020 forced so many kids online and on social media because they could not interact with one another in person, depressive symptoms and suicidal ideation increased in my practice. I witnessed a large decline in mental health due to the isolation and lack of motivation.

It is imperative that we understand suicide's relation to a lack of ability to manage difficult or painful feelings. My friend Leslie Weirich, a suicide prevention speaker and author, says that we can live a long time without food or water, but we cannot live without one second of hope. She states, "It only takes one second of hope to be here tomorrow."[57] Many children today don't feel they can solve their own problems. Things made too easy for them for too long have created a life for them that when something is hard, they don't know what to do other than to die. I have heard this from more kids over the years in psychotherapy practice than I care to count. So many children lose hope that their painful feelings are temporary, that they have the answer, that they can help themselves or find the help they need.

Another issue that is occurring because children and not made to be uncomfortable is a constant need to feel good. This has led to addiction. Young people are avoiding their pain by numbing themselves with substances. Drug use among eighth graders rose 61 percent between 2016 and 2020. One in eight teenagers abused an illicit drug in 2023, while 62.8 percent of twelfth graders who used marijuana in 2023 consumed it via vaping. Here's the real staggering number: Overdose deaths due to opioids have increased 500 percent among fifteen- to twenty-four-year-olds since 1999.[58]

Five hundred percent! What is happening to our kids? Their drug addiction begins long before they are exposed to drugs. It begins in preschool for the kid given an iPad to learn their ABCs. It begins at eight for kids who are given a smart device with access to the Internet, apps, and whatever they want at their fingertips. It begins when kids learn to check out. They check out on devices long before they are introduced to drugs. They miss the development processes they need to work through hard things. To work through discomfort and negative feelings. They are being trained to check out. It's not a huge jump to go from being addicted to the dopamine provided from technology to drugs and alcohol.

What is it going to take? Step up, parents. Stop giving children addictive devices while their brains are still developing! We have big problems, and we need strong adults to solve them.

If phones are the problem, take them away, delay usage, and say no, at least until you've figured out how to help your kids learn to be uncomfortable. Let them make mistakes, fail, learn, and grow. We should be concerned about their feelings but not to a point where we don't allow them to have any negative feelings at all. Negative feelings shouldn't be pathologized and diagnosed. They are normal.

Technology robs our kids of the discomfort required for development
Avoiding negative feelings is causing major mental health issues. Not moving through anxiety will cause panic disorders; not working through depression will cause self-harm and suicidal thoughts because kids will feel desperate to get rid of their pain. This is evidenced by emergency

rooms overflowing with mental health cases. ERs aren't equipped to manage this—it's not what they are designed for. More than 160 million Americans[59] live in a location where the mental health infrastructure cannot meet the demand. The mental health system was broken before the demand exceeded the supply and has fallen woefully short for decades. The weighted number of visits to ERs for adolescent mental health issues increased from 4.8 million to 7.5 million between 2011 and 2020—that's more than 13 percent of all emergency room visits among youth, per the report.[60] Suicide-related visits have increased from 0.9 percent to 4.2 percent of all pediatric visits.[61] There is nowhere for them to send these kids, as child psychiatric facilities are so sparse that children are sent home.

The phenomenon of school avoidance

As the school year approaches, it's not uncommon for many students to experience a surge of anxiety. For some kids it can feel much like the Sunday night blues, but others feel downright panicked about the return to school. So what exactly fuels the struggles that so many children encounter during the academic year? The roots of back-to-school anxiety largely stem from the modern generation's desire for comfort. Let's face it, school is demanding and frequently uncomfortable. Students are regularly juggling numerous social and academic pressures. They navigate the delicate art of impressing teachers, maintaining good behavior, staying organized, enduring long periods of sitting still, limiting device usage, cultivating patience, and navigating intricate social dynamics.

If a screen is overused in these years, it can wire the user's frontal lobe for addiction and prevent impulse control to keep the addiction under control. Screens wire the brain for addiction.

In contemporary times, the phenomenon of school avoidance is on the rise. This range of behavior can encompass outright non-attendance, habitual skipping, or even instances where students make it to school but struggle to last the entire day—resulting in calls to parents or frequent trips to the counseling office. Disturbingly, prior to the 2020 lockdowns, approximately eight million students were chronically absent from school. I saw this in my practice as kids increasingly became addicted to their devices and avoided hard things because of the constant dopamine surge they were getting at home using a device. School is hard but being home on a smartphone is not. Since the lockdowns, this number has doubled, with a staggering sixteen million children now showing signs of school avoidance each year.[62]

The lockdowns reshaped the educational landscape, making kids even more comfortable at home. Learning from one's bed while cameras are off, attending classes virtually, ordering food at a whim—these adaptations made staying home more appealing than ever. The integration of technology demonstrated to students that a multitude of activities could be pursued with ease and no stress.

Unpacking the struggle with discomfort

Why do students struggle with discomfort in the first place? This predicament finds its roots in a blend of parenting approaches and the pervasive use of technology. Today's children often lead lives devoid of significant challenges and obstacles. Their reliance on applications and gadgets sometimes bypasses the need to engage their innate critical thinking skills.

Parents, educators, and school staff hold the key to nurturing an environment that encourages children to confront challenges head-on. The goal should be to guide them through uncomfortable situations, allowing them to navigate negative emotions. It's essential to accept that feelings of being overwhelmed, nervous, embarrassed, or disappointed are all part of the human experience. However, the real concern arises when these emotions are left unprocessed and unaddressed.

Educators need to know they don't have to reward every good deed or correctly answered question. Modern students have become accustomed to being rewarded for the slightest achievement, leading to a distorted sense of accomplishment. This behavior-centric approach often thwarts their ability to learn from failures and mistakes, crucial aspects of personal growth and development.

The power of failure and intrinsic motivation

Failure holds a vital lesson—it's a catalyst for innovation and improvement. Embracing failure instills the ability to approach challenges from different angles, fostering confidence and resilience. It's an integral part of development. Moreover, the reliance on external rewards conditions individuals to seek validation externally, undermining the intrinsic motivation that should drive them. I often ask children and teens to set their own goals, independent of the outcome. Goals such as "I want to do my best" or "I want to work hard." This is intrinsic motivation. An internal drive. It eliminates the fear of trying and failing because if your goal is to work hard and you *do* work hard, independent of the outcome you desire, you have succeeded. That's the mentality kids need to feel good. The bonuses and rewards will come to you.

We must stop villainizing achievement and demands for excellence because in doing so we are weakening the children. If we don't think they can do it, *they* won't think they can do it. Achievement is in the journey. It's the bonus to the hard work. We are robbing them of the journey by making it easy for them to get rewards, good grades, and trophies. And by doing this we are telling them it's OK if they don't want to try. If they don't want to put in the hard work. We have given them a false sense of what it means to achieve. Many children avoid hard tasks because their egos cannot tolerate failure. Parents, it's your job to help them work through this fear. It's OK to try, even to try hard, and still not get the result you want.

My friend Brandon Judd's story of being given a participation trophy demonstrates how little this is helpful to children. Brandon recalls, "When I was seven years old, I played on a local kids' basketball team. I was never that good at basketball. No matter how much I wanted to 'be like Mike,' I struggled to put points on the board. Despite my air balls and bricks, I still hustled hard because I wanted to be good. But I just wasn't—and I knew it! After the final buzzer on the last game of the season, the team gathered to celebrate. The coaches, one of whom was my dad, started distributing trophies to the team one by one. Each trophy had a descriptive player title on the front. The first trophy presented said, 'MVP,' and was awarded to the best kid on the team. He was the clear choice. He eventually went on to make a name for himself playing college ball. The next trophy said 'All-Star,' and was awarded to the player who was great at both offense and defense. He was an obvious asset to the team. More trophies were given out: 'Best Defender,' 'Most Assists,' 'Free Throw King,' and so on. I looked at the table that was once full of trophies dwindle down to just one.

I'm the only one left—that one's gotta be for me. I wonder what it says? I thought to myself as the coach grabbed the final trophy and looked my way. I stood up from among the semicircle of players sitting courtside and walked toward the coach as he called my name. As soon as I was close enough to read the inscription on the trophy, my heart sank with embarrassment. 'Mr. Hustle'?! The coach made an attempt to spin this to sound like a good thing, but it felt like he had just given me the 'Bless Your Heart' award. I could almost hear the conversation the coaches had been having behind the scenes when deciding to give me this moniker: 'We're all out of compliments to give out.

What do we give the kid who's not very good, but he tries hard? I've got it! Mr. Hustle! Perfect.' I quietly returned to my seat, hoping that nobody would think too hard about my trophy inscription. Thankfully, nobody did, and this experience quickly faded into a distant memory."

Brandon reports, "To this day, I still remember how insulting that felt! As I matured and reflected on it, I realized my embarrassment came from knowing that we all knew I wasn't good, which I was OK to admit. But it was *more* insulting to me that they didn't think I could handle knowing that I wasn't good—and that they didn't think I was self-aware enough to recognize that!"[63]

If kids get a good grade or the trophy, we think they will feel good about themselves. Those are extrinsic motivators, and they are never enough. They aren't enough to fill the void of their lack of feeling capable. Parents do this because of our own misgivings about ourselves. A projection from our failures. I think Brandon's story tells us so much about how kids feel when we send them the message that we don't think they can handle the disappointment. If you push yourself out of discomfort, face your fear of failure, you can do the same for your child. Demand excellence, but from intrinsic motivators. Set goals for yourselves and them. Have individual personal goals, and then develop family goals.

Giving rewards without work is not the way to raise children. The generations of "everybody wins" and participation trophies have experienced a veiled attempt to build their self-esteem. If they get a bad grade, they need to live with the failure. Failure is necessary. Failure is how we learn. It is a gift. We must work through it and build ourselves back up. Life doesn't always give you second chances; sometimes it does, but not every time. What are we teaching our children when we allow them to re-do their failures? They aren't learning how to be motivated by what they want; they are being trained to get the reward.

What have we done to Generation Z? We've crippled them. During the 2021–22 academic year, among college-age people, 44 percent reported symptoms of depression, 37 percent experienced anxiety, and 15 percent seriously considered suicide.[64] This doesn't have to be. We have told them you get second, third, and fourth chances in life. We have told them you don't have to work hard. We've told them that the adults in their life will make sure they succeed, and they don't have to learn necessary life skills. We've taken away their autonomy. We haven't allowed them to *fail*. Failure is good. It's necessary for learning. For tolerating the discomfort of trying and just not getting the result they want. For developing the life skills they need to function in the world. Allowing them to fail will give them the confidence to go out in the world and be their best selves!

"Dreams demand hustle."

This is on the wall at the gym where my daughter practices gymnastics. I must have read this a dozen times without thinking much of it until one night while I waited for her class to end. I read this inscription on the wall and realized this gym does not give the kids candy at the end of their classes. Have you noticed everywhere kids go and everything they do, they are rewarded with candy? They get a haircut—candy. They answer a question right in school—candy. They go to a class or extracurricular activity—candy, or cookies, or cupcakes.

This constant reward feedback loop is conditioning children to think they will be rewarded simply for doing their job. That's not how life works; we don't get rewards for everyday tasks. We get rewards when we put the hard work in, and sometimes not even then. It's important our children learn how to be intrinsically motivated and feel good about their accomplishments on the inside, which will lead to more contented adults.

Dreams demand hustle, and you don't get a piece of candy every time you do the hard work. Doing the hard work gets you self-satisfaction, agency, and confidence—rewards that come later, internal rewards that are more valuable than sugar and artificial flavoring.

The reward feedback loop is ever present as kids continue to get participation trophies and sugary rewards for answering a question correctly in school. When kids are trained to get a reward for everything, they lack the ability to experience failure. When they fail, it renders them paralyzed. They don't know how to be disappointed, pick themselves up, and learn from it. They are being shielded from these opportunities to learn because they are constantly given "attaboys" and "attagirls" for not doing anything extraordinary. This erodes their confidence and self-trust.

Guiding children toward resilience

Parents and educators must allow students to navigate their natural developmental processes. The other side of discomfort is a place of empowerment, self-assuredness, and confidence. These are life skills that pave the way for success beyond the classroom. The path to overcoming back-to-school anxiety is through embracing discomfort and utilizing it as a catalyst for growth. By fostering a culture that values resilience and the ability to handle challenges, we equip the next generation with the tools they need to thrive academically and personally.

Just do it

I often think about the Nike slogan "Just Do It." Have you ever thought about this? It's a brilliant slogan. Working out and exercising has saved my mind. For me it's better than any therapy, meditation, massage, sauna, or any other healing modality we use these days. Showing up every day to move my body, work through the idea that I didn't want to do it. I told myself to *just do it* because I knew it would help me to feel good, and then I learned why from a neuroscience standpoint.

I urge you to be mindful of something I learned from Dr. Andrew Huberman. He was talking with David Goggins, an athlete and former Navy Seal who runs ultra-marathons of over one hundred miles. Goggins talks about the mind and how you can train it to do anything you want to do, but you must allow yourself pain and discomfort. Dr. Huberman shared with him about a part of the brain that grows when we do something we don't want to do. Something hard. It's a brain structure called the anterior mid-cingulate cortex, and it is especially large or grows larger in people who see themselves as challenged and then overcome the challenge. It's the seat of our will to live. We can build it up, but if we don't continue to do hard things we don't want to do, it doesn't grow.

In response to this, Goggins said someone told him he was blessed with a strong mind. He said no, I was not blessed, "That's something you have to develop." You develop it by showing up to your life every day. There are no hacks. You must do the hard thing repeatedly, until you "override your pain." It's the scientific explanation for willpower. In the interview Goggins said, "Build your will. Your will, your heart, your guts, your determination."[65]

As I was listening, I thought, *These are adults talking about learning this over time.* Dr. Huberman, a neuroscientist who had just learned this recently, had no idea of the anterior mid-cingulate cortex part of the brain. What valuable information for parents to teach their children. Such a gift. Stretch them, challenge them, grow their willpower, grow their brains!

KEY TAKEAWAYS

- ▶ Boundaries are important to establish with children to allow them to have their discomfort.
- ▶ Avoidance of painful feelings can lead to major mental health issues.
- ▶ Technology is increasingly causing dysfunction among today's generation.
- ▶ Parents must do the hard things and provide their children with discipline to help them grow.
- ▶ We grow when we do hard things.

CHAPTER 10

GENERATIONAL DIFFERENCES

If you look deeply into the palm of your
hand, you will see your parents and
all generations of your ancestors. All of
them are alive in this moment. Each
is present in your body. You are the
continuation of each of these people.
—THICH NHAT HANH

"DO AS I SAY, NOT AS I DO" IS A PHRASE MY GRANDMOTHER and my mother used to say, along with, "Mothers are always right, even when they're wrong." I would always point out to them how funny it was to me, the hypocrisy, but they were serious about it. They felt that being adults entitled them to do things that I wasn't allowed to do. It makes me smile now, looking back on our conversations about parenting. In each generation the parenting pendulum swings to the extreme on either end. We parent out of our wounds from the way we were parented.

I have noticed I am obsessed with modeling good behavior for my children. I find myself perhaps being too careful of how "good" I am in front of my kids. My daughter has expressed to me several times she thinks I'm a perfectionist. I say I'm a "recovering perfectionist" and assure her it's OK to make mistakes. Maybe I could use a little of that perspective from my mother and grandmother sometimes, acknowledging to my kids that because I am an adult, I can do things that I do not allow them to do. There is a psychological framework called the "good enough mother," coined by Donald Winnicott, that has helped me with this.[66] I thought I had to be a perfect mother until I learned that there *is* no perfect. There is *good enough.* If we show up every day, we are good enough for our children. Imperfections and all. They need us to make mistakes, learn from them, and try again. It's how they learn to do the same for themselves, through our modeling. There is a balance. The pendulum doesn't swing.

It's a bit of a boundary, isn't it?

The pendulum swing

When I talk about generational differences affecting the psychology of parenting practices, I use the analogy of a swinging pendulum. If we parent out of our wounds, rather than out of a connection with our child and their needs, we tend to do the opposite of what our parents did. Adjusting your parenting to what you didn't like as a child is healthy and natural. So is doing what works for you. It's called finding a balance. If you are not self-aware enough, you risk parenting at the opposite end, which is not good for your children unless you were severely abused and neglected. Even then, doing the opposite isn't healthy. For example, if you were abused you want to make sure you don't abuse your children, but you can't protect them from experiencing discipline and firm boundaries. You can do that with love rather than fear.

What makes a pendulum continue to swing without stopping in the middle? Weight. The heaviness at its end pushes it to the opposite swing. As parents, we are weighed down by our own projections that are happening as we raise our children, on top of all the pressures of parenting in today's times. It's enough to disconnect us and perpetuate the swing. The answer lies in you, the parent. Work on yourselves, on your heavy hearts from your own childhoods. We must stop the pendulum from swinging so far. Come to the middle; give this generation the gift of balance. The thing about the middle is that, in our wounding, we find it threatening because it feels dangerously close to the other side, the side we don't want to be. Giving your kid all of what you wish you had, and nothing of what you hated growing up, will create the opposite shade of the same problem.

When I was growing up, my mother cleaned the house every Friday. I remember coming home from school and cleaning my room because that was my chore. My mother had five kids, and I wonder how she did it all with minimal help from us. She didn't expect me and my siblings to do chores. I did them anyway because I knew they had to be done, I saw how overwhelmed she was, and I wanted to help. I recently asked her why she didn't require us to do more, such as asking my brothers to mow the lawn. We had a big backyard, and all four-foot-eleven of her mowed it herself. She shared with me that her mother had required her to do more than she should have at a young age. Out of her wounding, she didn't want to have the same expectation of us. This is a perfect example of the pendulum swing, of parenting out of your wounds. And while I don't always get the balance right, the pendulum in our family is in the middle. My expectation is that children be responsible for themselves and be of service to the family, and when my son tries to shirk his responsibilities of cleaning up after dinner by saying he has homework, my husband and I don't let him get away with it. We explain that we are a family, and we work together and help one another. If we do it together it will go quickly, and he can get right back to his homework.

Let us all be aware of ourselves; it is in our emotional immaturity that we aren't allowing our children to grow up. To do the independent tasks of childhood. We need to foster that awareness in them. What are you extreme about? How does your pendulum swing from the way you were parented? What is the middle for you? I'm asking you to reflect on that as a parent. Your children will benefit from that introspection.

The Greatest Generation (born 1928–1945) was raised with a stiff upper lip and the understanding that children should be seen and not heard. Their basic needs were met by their parents, but they did a lot on their own. They were resourceful, resilient. They were born during the Great Depression and World War II and were raised by parents who did what they had to do. Their parents were survivors. They had to be. There was no time for feelings. They were overdisciplined.

> Parenting out of your wounds will break your connection with your child. It causes them to propel away from you, like opposite ends of a magnet.

Their children, the baby boomers (1946–1964), rebelled against their parents' compliance. They wanted the opposite. They wanted freedom, no discipline. Their emotional immaturity didn't allow them to see that going too far wasn't healthy either. Hippies were looking for a connection to themselves that their parents didn't have or give to them. They were lost and disconnected, searching for meaning in drugs and sex, but they never found it. They went into parenthood disconnected from their children, Generation X (1965–1980), because their parenting was like their parents'. *The kids can fend for themselves, they are fine, let's not overanalyze anything.* I was born at the end of Generation X, in 1979, and my parents are boomers. As I came of age and thought about a career and having a family, my mom would say, "Your dad and I never talked about any of this, we just did it. Your generation thinks too much!"

Generation X was a product of the second wave of feminism, dubbed the latchkey generation or the forgotten generation because their mothers went to work, and the children were left to figure out their lives on their own. Feminism sold my generation of women a dream, telling us we could have it all, bring home the bacon, and fry it up in the pan. The baby boomer generation heard that message loud and clear. They went into the work force without an understanding that there had to be a balance between work and kids. The mentality was *the children will be fine*. There was no talk about "safety." We Gen Xers didn't wear helmets, have car seats, or chat on cell phones. We explored the world on our own, made mistakes, got into trouble—and no one was the wiser. We were thrown into the deep end and told to swim.

The balance for the baby boomers and their Generation X children *should* have been: Allow children the freedom they had, learn how to be resourceful, figure things out on your own, take responsibility for yourself, be free, don't obsess about safety. *And* ... we will teach you how to take care of yourself, solve your own problems, learn to be independent early on. You don't have to be thrown in the deep end to learn how to swim; we will teach you. Also, we want to know how you feel, and we want to help you work through your feelings of discomfort, not to fix them but to work through them.

For example, if you are concerned about allowing your child to ride their bike or walk across a busy road, you can explain that even if the signal tells you to go, you still must look to make sure cars are abiding by traffic laws. You can't trust the drivers, but you can trust yourself. This helps children feel agency and gives parents peace of mind to know their children can keep themselves safe.

But that balance didn't happen. Looking back, the kind of independence I had growing up is inherently good, and I advocate for it. Every generation before the millennials had free-range, independent childhoods. The issue with Gen X, though, is that our feelings were treated as if they didn't matter. The pendulum had swung away from the Greatest Generation women who did what they were told—the quintessential 1950s housewives. Many of them were unhappy and felt trapped. While I'm sure there are exceptions to these generalizations I am making, this can be said for the majority.

The daughters of those 1950s housewives rebelled against the notion that they didn't have a choice. Not wanting to repeat the same patterns as their mothers, they went to work. Naïve to the fact that their children needed them because "women weave the social fabric of society," according to Anya Pechko.[67] The women left the children, and the children felt neglected. Boomer mothers didn't know how to show up in that way because they didn't have that from their mothers. The parenting practices toward Generation X kids are indicative of the way the Greatest Generation had parented. Stiff upper lip, no one cares about your feelings; get over it; if you are sad, mad, or have any negative feelings, go to your room, and come back when you are happy.

I am a working mother. In no way am I saying women shouldn't work. What I am saying is that we should not have been told we could work *and* be happy without planning with our partners how to raise the children together. What happened to women is that we went into the workforce thinking it would make us happier than it did our mothers. It didn't. It made us exhausted because we were taking on most of the household and childcare tasks. Men didn't know what their role was. They shut down, feeling lost and not needed. This pushed women further into burnout. Women stopped helping one another with the child-raising. They went to work and thought they had to do it alone.

Divorce became common among boomer women in part, I think, because of this relationship dynamic. Even more recently, baby boomers continue to divorce more than any other age group. Between 1990–2012 the divorce rate for people ages 55–65 doubled. After 65, it tripled.[68] This was dubbed "gray divorce" because so many boomers were getting divorced later in life after they had grown children.[69] Generally speaking, they were dedicated to raising the children together—and they were also very unhappy.

Technology changed everything

The baby boomers also parented the millennials (born 1981–1996). Though the same generation parented Generation X and millennials, the two groups are very different. Millennials were the first generation to be parented with the philosophy of participation trophies. Talk of safety and making children comfortable was starting to enter the landscape. My family of origin was comprised of five children ranging over a ten-year age gap; the older three of us are Gen X and the younger two are millennials. My mom noticed the change among parents with my youngest brother, who was born in 1988. She remembers parents were yelling at coaches for not putting their kids in the game, making their kids comfortable, advocating for their children, and fighting the school on discipline issues by the time my brother was coming of age. When the older four of us were growing up, none of that was happening.

There was a touch of it in my sister's grade (born in 1983). The school all five of us attended was K–8, and upon eighth-grade graduation a scholar–athlete award was presented to one boy and one girl. The award commended the students for getting good grades while succeeding in athletics. It was a special award, and our school was always abuzz with who was going to win. By the time the awards were given to my sister's grade in 1997, there were multiple winners. The award lost its meaning.

What happened in that short time span from 1983 to 1997? The younger boomers had something different to contend with than their older boomer counterparts. The Internet! This is when AOL Instant Messenger came on the scene. Children were suddenly figuring out how to talk to one another through a screen without parental supervision or any education about cyber-citizenship.

Also, video games were becoming more popular. I remember us Gen X kids had Nintendo, but we only played it for small amounts of time and did other things. My youngest brother's generation played it for hours and hours, and the content started to become negative. I was with my mom at the video game store one day and she was buying him *Grand Theft Auto*. I was in college by then, and I told her my friends played that game, and it was not for kids. You could pick up prostitutes and see depictions of murder in the game. She had no idea. She'd raised us to be free-range kids. She didn't think she had to monitor my brother's technology use.

Many boomer parents with that same mindset raised their millennial children on tech. Overall the boomer generation, the first to experience television sets in their homes, didn't think the technology millennials were being exposed to was damaging. They were used to new innovations and adjusted well. It was like the urban legend of the slow-boiling frog. TV to them represented connection as many families would watch shows together, and because there were only a few channels, their peers watched those same shows. They could talk about the shows with one another and build commonalities. To boomers, the TV was positive. It enhanced the family dynamic. They had no idea what was coming. Their high tolerance for TV evolved into the era of twenty-four-hour cable.

Looking back, I think that was a slippery slope. What boomer parents of millennials didn't see coming was just how much the Internet and streaming TV would change how their millennial children functioned. As they came of age, the millennials were beginning to look a little like today's Generation Z. Certainly better, because they didn't have as much, but their functioning started to deteriorate. My youngest brother recently told me that he didn't use the phone as much as I did, and to this day he is anxious to answer a call whose number he doesn't recognize. This is because he didn't have as much social interaction, interfacing with adults, peers, and strangers, as I did. Much of his interaction was behind a screen. The millennials went to college with laptops and were in front of a screen during class. Professors lamented how difficult it was to keep their attention. It was benign compared to Gen Z but it still should be noted because parenting began to change with the millennials. Since they looked weak, the parents felt they had to keep them safe, help them, shield them from discomfort. Technology literally changed their psychology, and the parents changed right along with it! We haven't stopped parenting this way since, and the more technology is available, it seems, the more dysfunctional children are becoming. Parents are overwhelmed and don't know what to do because it seems out of control.

Remember when the millennials entered the workforce? No one liked them! Employers were baffled at how entitled they felt. They were labeled the "me" generation and called narcissists. Looking back, they were tame in comparison to Gen Zers. Nonetheless, they were the first generation to be this way, and the workforce didn't know how to manage it.

What did Generation X do with their Generation Z (born 1997–2012) children? Swing the pendulum the other way again! I am all about entrepreneurship, and because of this I think kids should work when they are young. Gen Xers are making life too easy for their Gen Z children because we feel wounded that it was hard for us, and we are not requiring them to work. I see so many teenagers who look good on paper—straight As, good athletes, will probably get into a good college—but they don't have part-time or summer jobs. I heard about a CEO who is known for hiring top-notch people. When asked how she hires them, she said she asks one question in interviews: How old were they when they had their first job? She doesn't hire them if they say anything over age eleven. At eleven children can't get a W–2 type job because of child labor laws, but they can walk the neighbor's dog, mow lawns, or babysit. My neighbor hired my son when he was around that age to cook her family's dinner! This is so good for kids! It teaches them a good work ethic, fosters responsibility, and builds their confidence, all of which keep children grounded in themselves and their connection to others.

Generation Z is entering into the workforce with even more gusto than millennials. Culturally, young people have lost respect for the older generations. Gen Z has coined the derisive phrase "OK, boomer." They are dismissive of baby boomers and their potential wisdom. There is no respect because they think they know everything. They are touted as a smart generation, but it's because they can find pages and pages on websites and YouTube videos on a subject they want to know about. They do have more information at their fingertips than the rest of us ever did; this is true. However, they stand to lose the wisdom and knowledge of older generations that you cannot find on the Internet. Due to this, Gen Z resists feedback from mentors and bosses. They are increasingly offended.

Gen Zers also tend to be unable to function socially. Offended by common constructive criticism in the workforce, they make complaints to human resources. It makes them so uncomfortable to hear that they're not perfect, that they have something to learn, that they may have made a mistake. Their narcissism, due to fragile egos, doesn't allow them to experience any negative feelings about themselves. This is a result of their parents not allowing them to tolerate discomfort.

Narcissism is born out of insecurity. A person develops a grandiose self-image to cover up a lack of self-confidence. How do children get confident? By doing hard things. Things their parents didn't make them do because they were kept comfortable. Take their need for "safe spaces," an unreasonable expectation—it's not the world's job to make them comfortable. We are only responsible for ourselves. This is the result of not allowing children to experience the messiness of their feelings along the way, with any hint of discomfort being extinguished by their parents, who didn't want to experience the pain of their children in pain. Thus, Gen Zers have never learned to process negative feelings. They are asking for emotional safety from the outside world because they don't know how to give it to themselves. Emotional safety doesn't come from the external. It's a feeling in your nervous system. If you can regulate your feelings, you can have control over your triggers of what comes up when someone says or does something to upset you. A regulated nervous system requires you to be able to work through your feelings and calm your body; it does not require the world to make sure you don't feel pain.

While it may seem like I don't like this generation because I talk about them so negatively, I care for them very deeply. You can think of it as "tough love." My oldest child is Gen Z, as well as most of my therapy clients over the years. They will tell you my tough love has helped them function better and improve their mental health. It's what they need from us adults, firmness and love acting symbiotically.

Millennials, familiar with parents keeping them comfortable and safe, are engaging in gentle parenting with their children. Gentle parenting is meant to be what is known as *authoritative parenting*, which encourages love and discipline. It was coined as the most ideal form of parenting, one we should all strive for, and is one of four parenting styles that Diana Baumrind identified. Authoritative parenting advocates for firm boundaries as well as care and concern for the child's emotional well-being. This is the balance that we are all looking for. Baumrind's other three styles are *authoritarian*, which comes with control and not allowing the child autonomy; *permissive*, allowing the child too many choices, not having firm boundaries, and overindulging their every desire; and *uninvolved*, which are parents who are mostly absent. These are parents who neglect their children either emotionally and/or physically. The children of parents who neglect them feel emotionally unsafe because there are no guardrails as they develop.[70]

Gentle parenting is being misinterpreted as permissive parenting. So-called parenting experts tell today's parents that they should always take their child's side, even when they are wrong. Don't make your kids uncomfortable. If they have negative feelings, create safe spaces for them to express them. Allowing them to express their feelings at home with you as a safe person is great! The problem is that today's parents expect teachers, coaches, schools, and society as a whole to make their children comfortable. *Comfortable* is not the same as *safe*. So many parenting experts and psychologists are talking about attachment and how to manage your children's behavior because there is so much need for this type of help. We try to exert patience because we are told that's what our children need; this is true, but we lose our tempers because we think we must be gentle, permissive, and allow them to behave badly in and out of the home. Then our patience is tested because being permissive causes kids to have no respect for boundaries. There can be a balance. Parents should care about their feelings and allow them to have negative ones but don't rescue them. Hold the space so they can work through it with your love and support. They can have feelings, but they are responsible for learning how to manage those feelings, with your help. Outside of the home, don't expect that to be the case. It's not the school's job to make sure your child doesn't experience any negative feelings. Negative feelings are a part of life. We can't have happiness without sadness. Out of the darkness comes the light.

Why are today's parents doing their children's work for them? I see so many parents doing things such as messaging online chat groups because their teen was selling something to raise money for his sport. The mother was selling the teen's products to raise money rather than allowing the teen to go door-to-door himself. It doesn't end there; many parents of older Gen Zers are holding their hands through college and even accompanying them on their job interviews. What is this teaching them? It sends the message that things will come easily . . . until they don't, and when they don't, they won't know what to do. They will be so afraid of failure that they may become paralyzed. I have seen more and more college graduates living with their parents and staying unemployed for longer than they need to. We have all heard that the jobs are not as plentiful for college grads as they were when we all finished college. This is somewhat true. However, the young adults that I have counseled have expressed that they will not take just any job; they want the perfect job, the one that pays a lot of money. This is directly related to the fact that their parents did not allow them to struggle for anything. They do not have the same work ethic as previous generations because they haven't learned the tools to knock on doors and experience rejection.

I was coaching a mom of boys who said her teenage son is very forgetful and she found herself reminding him of things he should remember at his age. This was a side comment, not the main reason she came to see me. She wanted to see me because he was becoming angry and aggressive. This had become exhausting for her, and she didn't know what to do. I suggested that she make him responsible for remembering by allowing him to forget something and then solve his own problem. All by himself. For example, if he leaves something in a public place, he should call the establishment and arrange for a time to pick it up. Then he can either get to the place himself (if it's local) or arrange for one of his parents to drive him when it's convenient for the parent. The only rule was that he must take the initiative and organize the solution; it was up to him how he was going to remedy the situation. She told him about my idea, and he loved it! She was shocked because she thought that he wanted and needed her constant reminders. I told her this would help with his aggression. He was trying to exert power and control where he didn't have any. Mothers can separate from their sons by allowing them the natural consequences life brings. This builds their sense of strength and autonomy, and only then can they experience agency and self-trust.

I believe parents are not aware of the connection between what screens have done and their need to enable their children. Technology has rendered children dysfunctional. They lack social skills because they grew up behind a screen talking to their friends, not in person. They have trouble with critical thinking skills, often unable to make a simple decision without consulting their parents. And remember Penelope and her roommates from chapter 4? Phone calls are difficult for this generation. Parents are responding to this lack of ability to function by doing for their children and not teaching them how to do for themselves. Teaching requires modeling the behavior, doing it with them, and then letting them do it on their own. Learning is getting lost in the "*with* them" phase. Instead, many parents are doing it *for* them.

I've been thinking about today's college students and their mental health decline. Their independence is fractured. Then I started to think about myself in college. Well, first I thought about myself before college. I was a brooding, angry teenager, resentful of my high-achieving older brother. I had experienced some ACEs myself but not enough to warrant a trauma diagnosis. No one comes out of childhood unscathed, but I didn't deal with my wounds. I easily could have been diagnosed with a mood disorder if I were a teenager today.

I had a boyfriend during my senior year of high school whom I was madly in love with and very dependent on for my self-worth. The first week of college I found out he'd cheated on me. I was in so much pain, I thought I was going to die, and then, when freshman year ended, my dad put me to work. His parking company was (and still is) contracted to run the parking at the university I attended. By sophomore year I was managing the entire operation. I didn't think much of it at the time. I have a lot of respect for my dad and would never say no to anything he asked of me, so I just worked.

I enjoyed it! I was making friends, going to business meetings, hiring and firing people, and dealing with a large amount of cash at the end of every night. Also, my very busy entrepreneur father, who was always working when I was growing up, would come to Ann Arbor once a week for meetings and take me out to dinner. I loved those times with him! When I graduated my dad offered me a role in the family business, acknowledging how well I'd done, and to this day my dad and uncle say I was the best manager they ever had. One of the people I hired still works for them.

That experience completely transformed me. I felt good about myself. My dad trusted me with his business, so I trusted myself. And I rose to the occasion! Make no mistake, it was hard work. Have you ever had to work in a parking lot in the dead of winter with no gloves because you were handling money and gloves got in the way? Not fun! Too many of today's young people are told they are mentally ill, traumatized, overwhelmed, unable to cope. They are told this by the adults in their lives who do the tasks of development for them—parents, teachers, school administrators, doctors, therapists, and college professors.

They are not made to be responsible for themselves. They're given free passes to miss an assignment, be absent from school, and otherwise not function in the name of their "mental health diagnosis" that wouldn't exist if they had agency. I would have been one of them had I been born just eighteen years later! Now I'm here to tell the adults in their lives to stop treating them as if they aren't capable of more.

Because they are!

If you treat them like they can't do it, they won't do it.

It's a self-fulfilling prophecy.

If you're a parent today, chances are you've seen the movie *Home Alone*. Early on in that movie, the youngest child of five, eight-year-old Kevin, loses his temper because his family has upset him. He is punished by being told to go to his room for the night. His family oversleeps and, in a hurried attempt to get to the airport for an international family trip, they forget to include him, leaving him home alone. I feel this scene demonstrates the pendulum swing of the boomers, Generation X, and their Generation Z parenting.

When I watch this scene as an adult, it's so obvious what is going on with Kevin. His family completely ignores him and treats him as a nuisance. They tell him to pack his suitcase for their big overseas trip, which he hasn't the slightest clue how to do. When he displays anxiety, his older siblings criticize him. No one takes the initiative to help him make a list or give him some ideas of what he might need. No wonder he breaks and pummels his brother! As his brother falls over, what ensues immediately after is chaos. The entire scene shows the aftermath of Kevin's physical altercation with his brother. Milk is spilled all over the plane tickets and passports, which are needed for the next day, and soda is spilled on Kevin's uncle. As the uncle stands up, pushing back his chair, it hurts his son.

The parenting practices in this movie are indicative of the type of parenting Generation X had. We were generally ignored, treated as if we should know adult things but never taught adult things, so we had to figure it out ourselves. Our feelings were considered annoying. We were dismissed, not seen and not heard. We learned how to rely on ourselves and be independent. We were also taught our feelings didn't matter. Generation X parents, out of that wound, have swung the pendulum so far the other way that they can't bear it when their children have any negative feelings.

How would Kevin be treated today?

Today's parents would pack his suitcase for him, not requiring him to be responsible for anything, and thus not teaching him how to do it himself and hindering his independence. They would also order an overabundance of the pizza he likes and make sure no one else eats it, rendering him incapable of conflict resolution. Lastly, today's parents would excommunicate Uncle Frank from the family for talking to Kevin the way he did. I am in no way advocating for Uncle Frank. His comment, "Look what you did, you little jerk" was *not* OK. His point was reasonable though. It was important for Kevin to see how his outburst affected the entire family. It is also important to communicate that effectively. Something like, "Kevin, I see you're really upset, and I want to understand it, but you should know your reaction isn't OK."

I talk about generational differences in parenting because of how I think the culture around parents shapes children's attitudes and perceptions. Today's children are treated as if they aren't capable of anything and are constantly made to feel comfortable—the opposite of how Kevin was treated.

How would I coach a parent in this situation?

The answer lies somewhere in the middle of how Kevin was treated and how today's parents treat their children. I would require Kevin and his brother Buzz to clean up the mess. They both had a part in making it. Then I would take the time in all the chaos to sit and listen to Kevin about why he reacted so strongly, because I know it was coming from somewhere. I wouldn't put Kevin in therapy for some anger-management issue. His anger was justified; he just needs help refining it and communicating his needs.

Once it was communicated, I would empower Kevin to take responsibility for his part in packing for the trip. What can he do to get himself ready on his own? Then I would offer to teach him how to do the rest. That would require some patience and time most parents have trouble providing, especially today with technology being such a huge distraction. Lastly, his older siblings need a talking to. If they were my kids, I'd be livid and have a firm voice talking with them. They are leaders and mentors. They should be held to that standard. They should have helped their brother, not criticized him for not knowing what to do.

For the current generation, Alpha (2012–present), we have time to do things differently. Millennials, you are raising Alpha children. I see you. You are confused by all the parenting advice. You want to follow your instincts, but the "experts" are telling you otherwise. Here is what I want you to know: I find that you are the most cognizant of what digital technology can do to your children because you know what it did to you. I encountered a millennial couple at a party who brought tablets and headsets for their kids to use. There were a lot of kids to play with at this party and no reason for any of them to have devices. At one point, the parents were questioning whether they should allow their children to stay on the devices, as the children were becoming more dysregulated. I could tell they were struggling to make the decision, weighing their parenting instinct against the cultural norm. The parents eventually decided to allow the screens. We ended up leaving the party because my youngest was the last kid standing without a device.

Parents, I know you want to do the right thing, but you don't think you have the answers yourselves. You *do* have the answers. You know what's right. Follow your instincts. Don't let anyone tell you different. Not even me. No more pendulum swing.

KEY TAKEAWAYS

▸ Generational differences affect parenting due to the
   pendulum swing.
▸ Bring awareness to your tendency to do the opposite of
   what your parents did.
▸ The most ideal form of parenting is authoritative
   parenting, in which boundaries are combined with love.

CHAPTER 11

THE FAMILY SYSTEM

In family life, love is the oil that
eases friction, the cement that
binds closer together, and the
music that brings harmony.
—FRIEDRICH NIETZSCHE

"WHETHER OR NOT SIBLINGS GET ALONG HAS EVERYTHING to do with the parents."

This was the response I got when I expressed concern to my mentor about having two children. I wanted them to get along and love each other. What she meant was that parents have to facilitate a healthy family system, one where each member of the family does their part to function and regulate themselves. I wasn't sure if I would do a good enough job being a mother of two. I didn't trust myself enough at the time.

I loved my firstborn so much I couldn't imagine giving that much love to someone else. When I said that to my great aunt, she held up all five of her fingers of one hand and said, "Which one do you love more, which one would you want to part with?" Her point was you need all of them, and you love them equally for the different purposes they serve. As a parent you will serve a different purpose for each one of your child's individual needs. And my cousin, whose kids were grown at the time, said, "You have to adjust to doing what's best for two kids, not just one." This hit me like a ton of bricks! I shifted my mindset to learn to do just that.

It was a very hard adjustment and looking back I made so many mistakes and have regrets. Despite my mistakes, who did my youngest choose to bring to Special Persons Day at her school? Her older brother. Though he would have to take a morning off from school and work hard to catch up from classes missed, he accepted.

I guess we didn't do too bad of a job!

Parents are responsible for sibling fighting, but not in the way you think. Siblings are the first peer relationship we have, and a lot of learning can come from how to resolve conflict as well as how to have a reciprocal relationship and deep, meaningful connections. Parents often feel we must referee siblings' fights. Yes, at times when fights become physical, parents must step in. Otherwise, parents need to help siblings understand the conflict. The secret sauce in this is what I call "my part, your part." They each have a role in the family system. They must do their part to maintain a healthy system. This means taking responsibility for their role in whatever conflict has ensued.

My older brother and I fought incessantly all through our childhood and even at times in young adulthood. When we were kids I never (and I mean *never*) thought about my part. It was always (yes, *always*) his fault in my mind. I thought he was mean, arrogant, aggressive, and talked down to me. He received lots of praise and positive attention from our parents because he was so well behaved, helpful, and mature. I was mean to him in what I thought was retaliation but which was actually anger at myself. He was high achieving, and no matter how hard I worked I could never catch up to him. I was most of the things he was—responsible, mature, well behaved, and helpful. The difference was I was loud about my feelings. That made it harder on my mom, and my brother got more positive attention than I did as a result.

What I now know is that I was resentful toward him because his success made me feel inferior. I didn't see his extremely hard work, tenacity, and dedication. Even though we lived in the same house occupying the same space for eighteen years, I couldn't see it, because I wasn't looking. This caused a lot of problems for me not just in our relationship but also in my young life because I didn't know whether I would be successful if I just continued to work for something I really wanted. Would it be enough? I worked hard and got good grades, but still they were not as good as my brother's. I hadn't learned yet what I try to teach children and their parents: If you want something, you have to work for it and not give up. Even when it's so hard you think you might break. My brother knew that all along, even when he was a small child.

I wouldn't fully understand my part until years later when I was counseling a set of siblings in my practice. These siblings had a similar family dynamic to mine growing up, and the younger sister was like me in that she was resentful of her older brother. Recognizing that I could help her since I had helped myself with this issue, we worked on ways she was contributing to the conflict; what she could do about it; and how she could find activities and interests that made her uniquely *her* so she wouldn't compare herself to her brother. This was a process, and along the way I saw myself in her. It caused me to realize just how shortsighted I had been about my brother. I apologized to him for the way I had treated him growing up. I don't think he ever expected to hear that from me but he was pleasantly surprised. Learning that you can't control anyone but yourself is so valuable, and when I was able to own my part, everything changed for me and for the relationship. There is so much power in that.

The family works like a system: If one person in the family is unhealthy, the whole family is unhealthy. And family systems are inherited. We either take on the roles of our parents, or we reject them so much that we go too far the other direction as the pendulum swings. The example we see growing up is so pervasive, we carry it into our own families and parent out of our wounds. Our birth order dictates the roles we take on so it's hard to resist what is natural. We don't always have to resist it. It's good to embrace a part of you that is powerful. You can use it for good, instead of dysfunction. Think of the family system like an assembly line. Each person in the family has their role. There might be the hero or "good" child that does everything right; the funny child who lightens the mood and makes everyone laugh; and the scapegoat child. The one who is trouble. The one who typically gets placed in therapy, on medication, or both. The family will be functional or dysfunctional based on every member fulfilling their roles. If one person changes their role, the family system is forced to change, rendering the family unable to function the way it had. We can't control whether a family member changes; we can only do our part by controlling ourselves. If we make changes, the family cannot operate the same way. For example, instead of your child being in therapy, you, the parent, can make changes to the family dynamic. If the system changes, the child changes. It's very powerful.

Children are like the canary in the coal mine. Coal miners used canaries in the early 1900s all the way through the 1980s to indicate any sign of carbon monoxide gas. Since the gas is odorless and colorless, coal miners would take canaries into the mines with them. If the canary passed out, that was an indicator to the coal miners to *get out quickly*. Canaries are sensitive, more sensitive than humans, so they reacted to the gas before the miners did. Children react quicker than adults; like canaries, their systems are more fragile than ours. They are more sensitive. They will react to the environment faster than us; you have your distractions and more control over your reaction. They don't have as many coping skills or built-up resilience yet. You can tolerate a lot. Especially now, with all the technological distractions available. We shouldn't be outsourcing the fixing of that—putting the "troubled" child in therapy. You don't fix the canary; you fix the air quality or the environment.

I have noticed a breakdown in the family system with today's fathers. Unsure of their role, they want to help but don't know how, causing mothers to feel alone in the parenting. The system isn't working. In previous generations, dads were the disciplinarians. When a child broke a rule or made a mistake, moms would say, "Just wait until your father comes home and I tell him what you did!" This was in the decades when it was more common for dads to go to work and moms to stay home with children, and because dads are generally better at discipline, especially with their boys. Moms nurture, dads provide the structure, and it scaffolds the child for growth.

Surely we have learned a lot from this type of authoritarian discipline; threats and fear don't work. However, it's the moms who have learned this because the majority of those reading the parenting books, going to the lectures, talking to their children's teachers, interfacing with their health care providers, arranging tutors, and scheduling babysitters are moms. It's more common today for dads to take on more of the child-rearing since both parents are working, so moms are relaying the information they get to the dads. In theory this "works," but what is actually happening is moms are not allowing dads to practice these skills. I see dads trying to discipline their children and moms stepping in because it feels uncomfortable for them, too harsh. This is often likely because Mom didn't have a balanced childhood of supportive authoritative parenting. Also, moms are being fed gentle parenting advice and are coddling the children. Dads don't like this, it doesn't feel right to them, but they don't want to challenge the moms because they trust they know what is best.

Many families are triangulating, which is a psychological term for a relationship dynamic. Mom and child are on one side of the triangle, dad and child on another, and mom and dad on the third side. We are only responsible for our side of the triangle, not the side with the other relationship. For example, moms are not responsible for a dad's relationship with the child. I see a lot of moms stepping in when dads are disciplining. This not only harms the father/child relationship, but it harms the side of the triangle with Mom and Dad. Moms need to allow dads to make mistakes and build their relationships with their children. Discipline doesn't have to be scary. It's OK for him to be firm. Let him find his way. He will stumble, but the children will survive that.

A couple I worked with, I will call them Regina and David, had a similar family dynamic to this description. David, the only child of divorced parents, was lonely as a child and wanted to do better for his children. He had attachment issues from being alone and was not close to his parents. He learned to rely on himself and thought he was doing OK until his oldest child was coming of age into the middle years around nine. David was resilient and had always survived. He was able to work hard and have a good job to provide for his family, but he was unfulfilled. He would often use alcohol to numb his disappointment in himself. He felt like he could do better and wanted to do better, he just didn't know how. Regina loved him and loved her family but didn't know how to reach David. She thought if she just kept the family afloat David would be happy and more present. She longed for his presence and was desperate to do anything she could to get it. She was enabling him. Her boundaries were not enough for her family to thrive, and she became resentful that David was not stepping up. This began affecting their oldest child.

David was not a strong male presence, and their oldest boy, I will call him Miles, was not feeling strong himself. He was getting picked on by other boys and did not know how to stand up for himself. David tried to coach him, but Miles was timid and afraid to hurt someone, as he was a sweet boy. Miles internalized shame that he wasn't strong enough and his dad was disappointed in him. He began acting out, displaying hyperactive behaviors that were annoying to the family and commanding negative attention. He was defiant, argumentative, and had trouble functioning. He was unable to remember to do basic things he was asked such as pick up his socks. Regina, alone in the parenting as David did not feel worthy of being present, coddled Miles and tried to fix what was broken. She didn't allow him to work through hard things. Both Regina and David reacted to Miles's behavior with anger, further shutting down his attention and focus and making the family *more* focused on Miles. He looked like the problem.

When a child is yelled at repeatedly, it triggers the survival mechanism in the nervous system, and executive functioning does not work. That "parent" of the brain is turned off to survive the situation, and the amygdala takes over. The amygdala is responsible for processing fear. Miles's behavior was causing stress to the family system, prompting them to seek treatment for Miles.

After meeting the three of them, it was quite clear to me that Miles was only reacting to the dynamic between Regina and David. I was not about to slap an ADHD diagnosis on him without working on healing the system causing his symptoms. So I worked with Miles's parents. I coached Regina to define her boundaries and keep them, and I helped David work on his underlying grief and depression. The couple began healing themselves and their marriage. Regina strengthened her boundaries, and David quit drinking. This clarity caused him to realize that he was more than he thought he was, and he lived up to his potential, gaining confidence in himself and instilling that confidence into Miles. Guess what happened to Miles? He became confident. He didn't like himself or the way he'd been behaving, so he did his part and worked hard to change his behaviors. He learned some jujitsu and defended himself against a kid who was physically hurting him daily. Miles also began getting more positive attention at home and did not feel the need to act out. His hyper-activity calmed because his nervous system felt safe. He stopped being the scapegoat and began defining himself in his true nature.

Miles has a younger sister, Jennifer, who was also affected by this dynamic in the way that she developed perfectionistic tendencies. She witnessed Miles often being disciplined for something and was on her best behavior. Not only did she not want to be in trouble with her parents, but she also didn't want to be a burden to an already stressful situation. When Miles stopped being the focus of his parents' attention, Jennifer was able to be herself. She was able to stop playing the role of the "good one" and began pushing back and being a typical child who makes mistakes. The entire family system had operated out of stress from the parents' past wounds. The system changed and the family thrived.

I see more dads wanting to be involved, showing up to my talks, asking questions, and participating in parent coaching. If you are a dad reading this, I see you and I know you desperately want to help your children. You show up because you want to know how you can be there for your children. Follow your instincts. You know what to do, the how takes practice. You are more important than you know. Research shows that when children are raised in fatherless homes, they are more likely to experience behavioral problems, poverty, go to prison, commit a crime, drop out of school, face abuse and neglect, and abuse drugs and alcohol.[71] They need you!

Who were you in your family of origin's dynamic? The hero? The jokester? The scapegoat? What worked for you in that role? Keep that. Then ask yourself what didn't work. Work through those feelings and let them go. You don't have to be that person anymore. Once you get clear on who you are and work through past issues, you can be healthy for your child. Everything aligns and you see them as individuals, not an extension of you. It's magical.

KEY TAKEAWAYS

- ▸ The family works like a system.
- ▸ Each person is responsible for their role.
- ▸ Parents are the leaders of the system and set the tone.
- ▸ Families need fathers; your role is important, and you can find a way to operate in the system.
- ▸ Encourage your children to see their part and ask them what they can do to help the system function.

CHAPTER 12

BIG TECH

*I believe that the abominable
deterioration of ethical standards stems
primarily from the mechanization
and depersonalization of our
lives—a disastrous byproduct of
science and technology. Nostra
culpa! (We are to blame!)*
—ALBERT EINSTEIN

TODAY'S CHILDREN ARE BEING OVERFED A DIET OF DIGITAL technology, otherwise known as social media, gaming, apps, streaming TV, and unfettered access to the Internet. I consider all digital tech to be under the same category, each modality responsible for one problem or another. At its core, these modalities are used to disconnect, to hide behind. Our children have become paralyzed and aren't able to manage life, devoid of coping skills and the ability to work through hard things. This desire for constant good feelings and the lack of ability to tolerate pain lead to myriad mental health concerns: addictions, eating disorders, self-harm, suicide, personality disorders such as narcissism and borderline personality disorder, gender dysphoria, and more. Online influencers try to make these illnesses look interesting and trending, and many children are wearing their mental health diagnoses as a badge of honor. They are overly attached to their diagnoses and are defined by them. This is a way for them to experience belongingness. Children are lost in tech. They've disappeared, it seems, but they are still somewhere in there. You can still reach them. You can reach them by first understanding what is happening.

Screenagers and the addiction to social media

This generation of teenagers has been dubbed "screenagers," a catchy name for the quickly changing development of their adolescence due to digital technology. The implications of this pervasive social media exposure include growing concerns about the well-being of this age group. Countless digital engagements—from YouTube videos and video games to websites to social media platforms such as Snapchat, TikTok, YouTube, Instagram, and Discord—constitute a substantial portion of screenagers' lives. This constant exposure subjects them to a barrage of messages that touch on diverse topics such as family dynamics, peer interactions, relationships, gender roles, sex, violence, food, values, and fashion, among others. Unfortunately, these prolonged digital interactions have not come without consequences. Observations have revealed a concerning trend of screenagers distancing themselves from their families and friends, often spiraling into disorders such as anxiety, depression, and addiction.

Notably, the severity of these disorders appears to be on the rise within this age group. Many young adults of Generation Z, beginning to recognize this in themselves, are opting for limited or no exposure to social media. They are trying to save themselves as their mental health declines. According to Jonathan Haidt in 2022, "self-reported depression among teenage girls between the ages of 12 and 17 has increased by 145% since 2010 to nearly 30% of all girls in this age group. For boys, it has increased by 161% since 2010, totaling over 10%. Rates of anxiety for adults aged 18–25 have also increased by 139% since 2010, according to the same dataset. By contrast, rates of anxiety for those between the ages of 26 and 34 or 35 and 49 have only increased by 103% and 52%, respectively."[72]

One notable manifestation of this phenomenon is the withdrawal exhibited by screenagers. Symptoms of depression emerge through their detachment from family, social activities, and hobbies that once brought them joy. This withdrawal tends to devolve into a cyclic pattern, wherein a screenager's sole source of happiness becomes the screen itself. Regrettably, the struggle to disconnect intensifies, leading to a troubling pattern of addiction.

So what precisely fuels the addiction among these screenagers? At its core, it is rooted in the pursuit of peer validation and connection. A prime example is the addictive drive behind sharing meticulously filtered images on social media platforms. Likewise, the rush of affirmation derived from gaining popularity through online bullying is a concerning aspect of this addiction. Moreover, screenagers are essentially addicted to one another—an interconnected web of mirror images seeking acceptance and love. In their digital personas, they can craft identities that cater to the approval of their peers. This virtual existence becomes a conduit for an imaginary audience, enabling them to be anyone they desire.

According to a UCLA study conducted at Ahmanson-Lovelace Brain Mapping Center,[73] the pleasure part of the brain lights up when teens play video games or use social media. In this study, the researchers scanned teens' brains while they were using social media. They found that the same brain circuits that are activated by eating chocolate and winning money were activated during social media usage. Specifically, they found that when screenagers see a high number of "likes" on their own photos or the photos of peers in a social network setting, the pleasure part of the brain becomes activated.

It's no wonder screens are referred to as "electronic cocaine" and "digital heroin." Screenagers whose parents have taken efforts to limit or eliminate social media altogether say their kids feel empty and would rather be cut off from the real world than cut off from the online world.

This is so telling. They are completely overly attached to the online world and not attached enough to real people and real life. The signs of addiction to look for in your teen include:

+ obsessive thoughts about video games, social media apps, and so forth
+ anger when the screen or video game is taken away
+ withdrawal
+ the inability to deal with life when things do not go their way
+ lack of socializing with peers and family members in person

More specifically, the addiction to screens works just as an addiction to alcohol, drugs, food, or gambling does. The brain's response to something that feels good is a release of the neurotransmitter dopamine. Dopamine is known as the feel-good neurotransmitter. Studies have shown that the touch of a screen, or even just thinking about a video game, leads to the release of dopamine and gives the person instant pleasure. A child does not know how to establish a boundary around this feeling and will want that feeling all the time. Over time this chemical response overwhelms the brain, and the brain's defense to being overwhelmed is to produce less dopamine. The screen then no longer gives them as much pleasure, so they engage more to maintain the pleasure. This is known as tolerance.[74]

This concerning addictive cycle can ultimately breed apathy—a sense of emotional detachment that educators and administrators are increasingly observing among students. Many educators report encountering students exhibiting signs of depersonalization disorder, a condition marked by emotional numbness and disconnection from their surroundings. Those grappling with this disorder often describe themselves as detached from their own bodies, leading an existence devoid of meaningful purpose. A clear correlation has emerged between this disorder and excessive screen usage. The disconnected way screenagers interact with the world during their development contributes to their physical and emotional detachment from their surroundings. The proliferation of screens and electronic devices has ushered in a new era of connectivity for screenagers, but it has also raised red flags about their emotional well-being. They exhibit a lack of concern for themselves or their futures and will often describe themselves as *living out of their bodies.*

The pervasive addiction to screens, driven by the quest for peer acceptance and validation, has the potential to yield dire consequences—ranging from depression and anxiety to suicidal outcomes. Acknowledging these issues and fostering healthy screen habits during adolescence is imperative to ensure a generation of youth equipped to navigate the digital landscape while maintaining their mental and emotional well-being.

It's not just social media that is addictive when it comes to technology. Big Tech, much like Big Tobacco, has intentionally made its products addictive. The algorithms used by social media giants have been created by people who know how the brain works and, instead of allowing each positive emoji and comment to appear as they are made, the algorithm collects them to give you one big burst of a dopamine bomb of validation at the same time. I called them "evil geniuses." They know our wants, our needs, our desires. They offer it so easily. I'm sure as you're reading this, you're imagining the ways Big Tech has gotten its tentacles into you. Imagine how your children are affected. Imagine just how stunted they are by tech.

Suicide pacts and personality disorders

Research shows there is a correlation of depression, self-harm, and suicidal outcomes in adolescents from social media use.[75] The social network is virtual; it's not real nor is it authentic. Even though we are aware of this, human beings have a deep need for connection. Belongingness, connection, and community give a sense of safety. Alternatively, loneliness causes illness. A Harvard longitudinal study on adult development followed men for eighty years beginning in 1938. They found that being socially connected to family, friends, and community leads to happiness.[76] More specifically, this connection is rooted in quality relationships where there is mutual secured attachment. This means that both individuals in the relationship feel they can trust the other with their vulnerability. These types of relationships led individuals to live longer, stay healthier, and even have better memory as they aged. In contrast, they found that poor human connection leads to loneliness, which leads to decline in health. These people lived shorter lives and experienced a decline in brain function.[77]

Furthermore, Vivek Murthy has raised awareness about a "loneliness epidemic." Loneliness and isolation are harmful to our health, factors that "increase the risk for premature death by 26% and 29%, respectively."[78] The need for connection is so powerful that it becomes addictive online because we never get enough validation, which we tend to mistake for connection. Since socializing online is not real, children try to fill a void—but to no avail. It doesn't work. It's not a real connection. Feeling good from the validation social media can bring is temporary. I often see adolescents who develop emotionally manipulative, attention-seeking behaviors in the real world from constantly seeking it in the virtual world. Except in the real world, it's harder to get, and the attention-seeking behavior leads to depression.

I was seeing borderline personality tendencies in my adolescent clients since social media began growing from Facebook to Instagram, Snapchat, and TikTok. Borderline personality is born from childhood abuse and neglect. At its source it is an emotional wound that manifests in a fear of abandonment. It comes with the inclination to self-harm, symptoms of substance abuse, and impulsive behaviors around sex and spending money. This disorder often includes suicidal ideation, threats, and attempts; mood fluctuations and irritability; outbursts of rage; and volatility. Relationships are unstable because of these extreme reactions. It is more common in girls and women, and my practice saw many adolescent and teen girls with symptoms of this disorder. However, they didn't have the psychosocial histories to warrant the diagnosis. What was at the root of their fear of abandonment? Online relationships that are seemingly real to them but feel fragile. The nature of the relationship online is superficial, so it's easy for someone to end it with the click of the "unfriend" button or by ghosting someone.

People with borderline personality disorder use emotional manipulation in their relationships to prevent those they love from leaving them. They read boundaries as rejections, which trigger their abandonment wound, and they will go so far as to self-harm and threaten suicide when boundaries are put in place. This is overwhelming for the people in relationships with them because they feel trapped. Many children harbor this burden on their own and do things such as stay up all night talking to their friend who is threatening to die by suicide. This is especially common among middle school and high school girl groups. They become toxic together talking about their mental health diagnoses, using their diagnoses to behave badly and treat one another poorly.

Many girls who fit this archetype have parents who are permissive and feed into this need for constant validation and good feelings. The parents do not allow them to be uncomfortable, learn conflict resolution, or work to be in a healthy relationship. They are not modeling a healthy relationship with boundaries, because they give in to their child's every demand. Their parents are literally afraid of them—afraid of their reactions if the parents say no.

Many of these girl groups enter "suicide pacts." When the attention they are seeking has reached a level of "not enough," they plan to attempt suicide. This involves the girls' taking turns, and if one survives and is in the hospital, another will attempt. They don't really want to die, but they certainly could. Then one gets out of the hospital and not only gets attention for their attempt but shows concern for their friend. It's a game to them—children playing Russian roulette with their lives. Their immaturity doesn't allow them to see its permanence. This isn't depression; this is a pathology created by social media. Though this sounds unbelievable, it's not. I have borne witness to it. I wish I could say I had only a few of these cases and that they were rare, but at one point, these cases filled my practice. I like to point this out to parents because the need for constant validation and subsequent reactions are character traits that develop during adolescence. If provided with boundaries, the personality traits can be undone before the child reaches full maturation at twenty-five. Boundaries are necessary if you see your child developing borderline personality traits.

Online dating

Snapchat was created for adults and has become normalized for adolescents and teens. They are using this app for dating. They meet one another through shared contacts on Snapchat, "snap" one another, and develop a superficial connection. Sexting is considered normal on this app; many kids are asked for nudes and end up sending photos of themselves to complete strangers. The girls' pictures are meant to convey their sexuality. They are often dressed seductively and have the quintessential "duck lips" pose to make them look sexualized. Hypersexualization of young children is becoming normalized as younger children are being exposed to social media.

Furthermore, it is becoming popular for children to buy drugs through Snapchat, Facebook, Instagram, TikTok, and YouTube. Ads targeting young people pop up and go away quickly. These posts use code words and emojis. A child comments on the post or private-messages the person. Then they move the conversation to WhatsApp, Telegram, or Signal and pay through cash apps. A few clicks later and dangerous, illegal drugs are delivered right to their door.

Social media apps such as Instagram also give way to sextortion. This scam targets boys by posing as a girl their age. He talks to her, gets comfortable, and then is asked to send a nude photo of himself. The child then sends a nude photo and the threats begin. The scammer asks for money; if they don't get it, they threaten to expose the child's nude photo to everyone they know. The child, not having their own money, feels trapped and, rather than face the idea of having their nude photo distributed, takes their own life. They don't feel they can go to their parents because of the shame of making this mistake. We must stop normalizing allowing children to be on social media. It is not safe, and parents should know what is happening.

Sexual exploitation of children is so pervasive that there is movement to change the language of child pornography to child sex abuse material (CSAM). We no longer call it child pornography because that vernacular isn't disturbing enough. Online CSAM is becoming popular as the social media giants Instagram and Facebook allow their users to view it. This begs the question: Should tech be regulated? I watched the congressional hearings for the Kids Online Safety Act (KOSA),[79] and I have some thoughts. First, I love that this conversation is in a mainstream space. I have been talking about technology's effects on child development for eight years. Second, I think it's too late! This conversation was needed ten years ago, and every day for the last ten years until parents understood how harmful these products are to their children. Third, there will always be a way around regulation. Parents, you need to know what is going on online and stay connected with your children.

Did we really trust Big Tech to keep our kids safe? They are in this for profit. How could we think they care about our kids? We, the parents, must take responsibility for allowing it. Big Tech simply tapped into something that was already there—disconnection and a lack of ability to tolerate discomfort. A lack of self-confidence, agency, autonomy. It's our fault. We have let this happen to ourselves and to our children! Who should care about our kids? The government? No, *we* should! The government has let big industries get away with harming us for years. Big Tobacco, Big Food, Big Pharma, and now Big Tech. These companies hook kids on their products as young as possible to groom lifetime users—the oldest marketing trick in the book! Have you ever thought about that word? *Users*. Addicts are called users. Big Tech is telling us by the name they use to describe us that their products are addictive. We should know better. What the government is doing now is a political stunt. If they don't act, they look like they don't care. And that doesn't serve them. Where were they ten years ago? They've been allowing lobbyists to line their pockets. The government isn't going to save us.

We must save ourselves.

Protect ourselves from Big Tech.

Protect our children.

Protect their childhoods.

Parents, it's your responsibility.

It's on you!

Don't let Big Tech infiltrate their innocence.

You don't know what you don't know.

And parents, once you know, you can be the powerful beings you are and protect your children!

Parents have power!

It's up to us!

Gaming

Boys have a proclivity for competition. It's biological. They are made to fight, but they aren't getting their needs met in this way. There is not as much competition for boys in school because they aren't given the opportunity to be competitive physically early. Girls are outperforming them as traditional school allows girls to succeed. This makes boys feel inferior, and they shut down. Out of concern for mental health, many of today's schools are not challenging their students. There are no consequences for not turning in assignments, kids are given free homework passes, tests can be retaken to get the grade you want, and projects can be redone. Low quiz and test scores are dropped to help a child along. The children are coming to school looking less capable, not resilient, unable to do hard things. By letting them take the easy way out, schools are enabling low self-esteem and fueling feelings of unworthiness. There is no need to be motivated even to try. No attempt to challenge themselves. This isn't black and white. I think if a child is working hard with their best effort, it can be healthy for them to ask a teacher for extra credit or to retake a test. That is a sign of perseverance. I am concerned about the boys who give up before they even try and then are given a free pass. They need to be challenged.

Boys are not getting their needs met in the real world, so they turn to online gaming to satisfy the need to be competitive. Gaming companies create algorithms to make it addictive in that way. In many games, there is a series of challenges that open doors to the next challenge once you've completed one. Life is hard for boys in the real world; they prefer to play a game that is designed specifically for their brains to feel good. The dopamine rush can't be paralleled in the real world, even for the boys who play a sport. They may get what they need from the sport, but they still aren't supported in their need to feel strong in other parts of their lives. The thrill of the competition in real-life sports is one piece of the puzzle. The other piece is that boys must take what they learned from sports off the court or the field. They can't avoid hard things such as school, talking about their feelings, or communicating in their relationships. Dr. Laura Markham writes, "Computer games change our brain chemistry while we're playing them, and we don't know how long the effects last afterwards. Kids do need our help to manage this addiction."[80]

A child I once worked with disclosed that the game Minecraft was addictive for him. He was ten. His parents, cognizant of how gaming could be problematic, reluctantly agreed to get him a game system with a long list of rules and boundaries. It wasn't in his room; it was in a common space of the house so they would know what he was playing, as violent video games were off-limits. He could not play online with friends, and his usage was limited to one hour per week. At first, he didn't play unless friends were over, but eventually he found himself wanting to play all the time. His parents were very intentional about making sure he used it appropriately, and this allowed him to have some awareness. He was able to come to me after a week and tell me he thought it was addictive for him. Why? Because he could create the "perfect" world online. The real world was not perfect for him. He knew this, and he knew that immersing himself in a fake online world that made him feel good wasn't the way to deal with it. We agreed he would take a break from Minecraft so he could reset and get himself to a good place in the real world.

The break from the game opened a door to discover what was really behind his desire to have a perfect world. He discovered that he was experiencing feelings of low self-esteem. He wasn't feeling successful in school as it had become hard for him. This was unbearable because he was told by the adults in life that he was smart. He was quite mature and could carry on conversations with adults. I could see why people thought this of him; he was very articulate, emotionally intelligent, and engaged well in his sessions with me. He also had a very creative mind and used his imagination to build elaborate LEGO structures. School didn't allow him to use these talents. He was required to sit still, listen to lectures, and memorize information. When school got hard, he questioned whether he was, in fact, as smart as his parents and extended family had always told him. In his mind, being smart meant you knew how to do everything and nothing was hard. Once this came out in his therapy, he was able to work through the difficulty of school and gain confidence from doing something hard. No more Minecraft addiction.

Though I was able to help him, this boy didn't need therapy. He needed his parents to recognize his addiction, take the game away, and create space to connect with him. They were supportive, loving parents who showed up and would have been happy to talk to him about his insecurities. Parents, I implore you to look up from your devices and see your children. They need you.

A school's role with technology

Who is responsible when children are on devices during the school day? It may seem like a chicken-or-the-egg question. Is it the parents sending their children to school with devices? Or is the school requiring a device for learning? When devices first came on the scene, schools tried to fight it. They had strict off-and-away policies, and there were consequences for kids who were using devices during class time. The parents fought those policies. Helicopter parents wanted to stay in touch with their kids all throughout the school day. Then the parents blamed the schools when things started getting out of control. Schools responded with policies that allowed phones during free time such as lunch and recess. They called these periods "red light" when the phones weren't allowed and "green light" when they were. That didn't work. The message to the kids was that the adults don't have this under control. We haven't figured it out. Schools, caving to the parents' pressure, began welcoming the devices. "If ya can't beat 'em, join 'em."

During this storm I gave a lecture at a local middle school. A mother asked a question at the end regarding the "green light" policies. She felt it was inappropriate to allow the kids to be on their devices with no supervision. The middle school counselor interjected and said, "You are the one paying for and sending your child to school with this device." That was the first time I ever heard a school official stand up to a parent. It was great, but it was still an isolated incident. I think school administrators, counselors, teachers, and anyone working with students have inherited a burden that should not be theirs to manage. Schools do not and will never offer enough mental health care to service the level of need. Kids are coming to school with nude photos on their devices, threats made on social media, suicidal threats made by their friends. This is heavy stuff for kids to manage without trusted adult help, and schools aren't equipped. Nor should they be. They are not mental health institutions; they are educational institutions.

The responsibility lies with the parents. Parents must stop fighting school policies that protect children from the disaster that tech has caused on child development. You don't need to stay in touch with your children all day. They need to navigate the world without you. It's good for them. Remember, separation happens at every stage of development in small bits. You must allow it, or it won't happen when it's supposed to in young adulthood.

UNESCO has recommended a ban on digital devices during the school day. They are urging countries to carefully consider how devices are used in education. They found that the mere presence of a smart device creates a distraction for students and negatively impacts learning in fourteen countries.[81] The pressure to respond to notifications is weaved into our culture, with children feeling stress and anxiety for leaving someone on "read." In their immaturity, they think if you don't answer someone, they'll believe you are upset with them. They lack the ability to have the conversation, so they don't talk to their friends about why there was no response, creating more stress and anxiety. Learning is not happening on devices, as was promised. Children are distracted in school and after school while doing homework. Education technology, aka ed tech, are modalities educators use to teach children online through overstimulating game applications. There are math and reading games that offer rewards at a certain number of points for answering a question right. The reward is a pop-up that says "brilliant" or "awesome." Apps for quiz and test preparations offer students the promise of making learning fun. I have noticed that these games are designed to give the user the reward feedback loop. It feels good to get validation after every correct answer. It's addicting and keeps the student engaged while playing, but they are not retaining the information.

Furthermore, some studies show this way of learning is not working. A longitudinal study of K–3 children demonstrated that ed tech has negative effects on learning achievement and contributes to the gap-widening effect. The gap-widening effect highlights educational inequality.[82] During the 2020 lockdowns, it became clear that ed tech was not as accessible to children in low-socioeconomic families. They were not able to access the Internet through Wi-Fi, and some didn't have laptops to Zoom with their teachers and classmates or complete assignments. Pen to paper stimulates the brain. It opens brain pathways and allows for creativity in a way that a screen cannot. When my daughter learned cursive writing, her teacher said, "Writing in cursive teaches the hand to have a sense of control." Having control over your hand is a physical manifestation of having control over yourself, something many schoolchildren struggle with. It can be very powerful to use your body to feel a sense of control.

Furthermore, if you think your school has effective safeguards, firewalls, limits, and rules regarding devices, you're wrong. Kids are smarter than adults when it comes to circumventing controls. Many schools have firewalls on their network that strictly filter inappropriate web content, but don't block a particular site. To get around that, kids are using their personal logins to access sites such as YouTube unrestricted. They search not safe for work (NSFW) sites on YouTube that bring up sexual images. Middle schoolers report to being on pornography sites in school during the school day! Many teachers have phone pockets on the wall for students to check their phones during class time. Some savvy students place an old smart device they found in a junk draw that hasn't been turned on in years in the pouch, allowing them to use their own smart device undetected during class time. They hide AirPods in their ears by putting their hands over their ears and slouching down. With the Bluetooth ear device, they listen to music, cheat on tests and homework, and are overall not present for learning. We have created tired and wired, unhealthy children and we wonder why there is so much attention deficit, depression, and anxiety in schools. They aren't disordered; they are falling behind because they aren't present. Their cognitive functioning is declining, and they are training themselves to not use their executive functioning. Hiring more school social workers and counselors and creating IEPs for children isn't the answer. The answer lies in understanding the root cause and changing the landscape.

Loneliness

We are more "connected" than ever online, so why are we experiencing a loneliness epidemic? Loneliness is particularly concerning because one of the greatest risk factors for suicidal outcomes is social isolation. When a child feels disconnected from the people in their lives, this can lead to loneliness, lack of self-esteem, apathy, and a lack of motivation. Often children will say, "What's the point?" or ask themselves questions such as, *Why am I here?*

What is this phenomenon, and why is it happening? Developmentally, children age nine and older begin to individuate and see themselves as people outside of their families. This is when friends become important to them. Adolescence is the peak of this development and when they need social interaction the most.

With today's technology, the perception may be that children and adolescents are connected to their peers more than ever. There are many positive experiences meeting peers online from other geographic areas. In a vacuum, this is positive.

However, the truth is that today's youth spend increasingly more time physically, emotionally, and mentally isolated from their peers. Oftentimes, devices and technology disrupt true connection with loved ones. Even when they are physically with their friends in the same room, they are on their devices showing each other memes and videos. The phone, central to all their interactions, creates a lack of balance between virtual socializing and real-time human interaction. In my practice, I see many children forming unhealthy attachments to strangers online and becoming further withdrawn from their real-life lives. Many children who have trouble socializing use social media as a crutch to avoid having to face real-life social interactions. It's more comfortable to converse behind a screen.

Socializing is already extremely uncomfortable for children and adolescents. They are uncertain of themselves, are just beginning to learn who they are, and must contend with what others think of them. Children need to learn how to interact with one another, taking the good interactions with the bad, learning how to manage the messiness of vulnerability. Allowing children to individuate along the way and build that connection to themselves without distractions helps them to connect to others. The idea is: If I can have me, I can relate to others. I have seen many children withdraw further inward from not allowing themselves to navigate hard situations. Today's parents struggle to be uncomfortable with their *own* feelings. As a result, they are unable to allow their children to be uncomfortable with theirs. The culture of parenting today is one in which parents overcompensate for children who don't want to face adversity and do hard work to overcome it. Parents strive to make their children's lives easier by doing things for them, creating a generation of children who look for the easy way out of such things as socializing with peers. It's important to their development that they work through the discomfort of uncertainty in themselves, not avoid this process behind a screen, as avoiding leads to depressed feelings that get stuck.

Lack of empathy: kindness is missing

Empathy has been decreasing among the iGeneration. The part of the brain that develops empathy is the frontal lobe, which begins developing at birth and does not stop developing until a person reaches age twenty-five. It is in the frontal lobe that we learn unspoken language such as facial expressions and body language. We also hear people's tone of voice and pick up on social cues from that. This is where we learn to interact with the world. When we touch a book at the age of one and point to the pictures, open flaps, and feel texture, that tactile response stimulates the brain pathways in ways that a screen simply cannot. If we are placing a two-year-old in front of a screen to learn her ABCs, and then a young child in front of a screen that reads him books, followed by the adolescent who has a smartphone, we are impeding those brain functions that are meant to develop naturally from stimulants in the environment. This can lead to the lack of development of empathy all the way into young adulthood, possibly forever. Neuroscientists are asking the question about neuroplasticity and whether the developing brain will be permanently affected by technology. Neuroplasticity is the brain's ability to grow through life experiences. We know there are critical periods of developmental windows that, in the right environment, cause the brain to grow. We don't yet know what happens to the brain when the environment is not nurturing to growth, as in technology exposure. The topic is one we should all think about, and the research may eventually tell us much more.[83]

We are doing our children a disservice to assume that technology is better than a mother's and father's voices reading their child a book, with tone and inflection. Listening to your parents' voices develops the brain's empathy pathways. If a parent and/or child is in front of a screen, eye contact and seeing facial expressions are reduced. Looking in someone's eyes and watching their expressions are ways to see the person in front of you. You can experience their feelings simply through looking at their face or their body language. There is an energy transfer when you really look at someone. A connection is made. Have you ever tried to merge into heavy traffic only to be frustrated that no car is letting you in? Have you noticed if you make eye contact with someone and motion to them that you are asking to be let in, they are more likely to let you in? It works the same with a screen. The device is the thing between you and the other person, preventing you from seeing each other. When we impede development with screens, we erode a child's ability to develop attachment and human connection. This is evident in the first stage of social emotional development, a child's ability to develop independence and autonomy, a lack of self-confidence (stage two), and a lack of purpose (stage three). When a child reaches school age, they will have no idea who they are or what they are supposed to do in life. This makes for depressed, anxious, apathetic children who continue to use screens to interact.

What does lack of empathy development look like? It leads to an increase in bullying. No doubt bullying has been around for generations. There is the bully who takes a kid's lunch money, the bully who fights after class in the schoolyard, and the mean girl making fun of someone for what she is wearing. However, the type of bullying happening on social media, known as cyberbullying, is beyond any kind of bullying that you and I encountered during our school years. That bullying does not end at three o'clock when school is over; it continues on social media all afternoon, evening, and even into the late-night hours, as teens stay on their phones. This type of cyberbully aggression makes a kid popular among today's youth. They lack social skills offline and only know how to interact with a screen between them. When one person in the friend group dislikes someone, the entire group then comes together and harasses the child online. Groupthink is more common among teenagers because they lack the skills to think for themselves, and their desire for conformity takes over.

The following are some examples of severe cyberbullying. When social media started, I learned through my teen clients that mean posts on Instagram were prefaced with "TBR," which stood for "to be rude." For example, "TBR—you're ugly" or even more alarming, "TBR—go die." It is a game to them. Someone insults someone, and the ante continues to be raised. This has been going on for more than a decade! These screenagers do not have any connection to the notion that when they say things such as "go die" and "why don't you just kill yourself already," there is someone on the other end of a screen receiving that message who feels it and takes it very personally. Teen suicide has occurred because of this type of bullying. According to the cyberbully hotline, suicide is the number three killer of teens in the US, following car accidents and homicide, respectively; 81 percent of teens say bullying online is easier to get away with; and 20 percent of teens cyberbullied think about suicide, while one in ten attempt it.[84]

What happens when *parents* are the bullies? There are videos on social media of parents pranking their young children, some of them as young as two and three. One ruse they tell the children is they are going to bake something and they ask the child to have an egg ready to bake with. They then crack the egg on the child's forehead and laugh. Watching these videos is quite disturbing; the child is left bewildered and confused, the joke going over their heads. Many of them start crying while the parents look at the camera and laugh. Some of these videos have received millions of views. The parents are clueless to how inappropriate this is. As I watched, I realized all the parents were young—either on the young end of the millennial generation or the older end of Generation Z. It occurred to me that these parents were raised on technology. Raised to be disconnected. Raised to lack empathy. How else could they show such complete disregard for their children?

Parents share pictures of their children online, a seemingly more benign practice than pranking your toddler. The pictures are often fun in nature: dance recitals, first day of school, and birthday tributes. I understand the draw; when my oldest was young I wanted to share everything about him. I was so in awe of him. I shared some, but not a lot because my instincts told me not to. Then when he was around four, my husband took a picture of our son and he said, "Don't share this online." I don't even know how he knew about social media and parents sharing pictures of their children. This can be an issue for children later in life. Their lives have been chronicled online for all to see, so some of today's teenagers and young adults are resentful of their parents. Quite common among today's parents is the term "oversharenting." We don't have permission to post pictures of them and share their lives with the world. They are not able to give us permission, and it's important that parents think about that; be intentional about what you share and how you share it. There is also a safety concern as AI becomes more sophisticated. Our faces can become anything to anyone. If you share a picture of your child, their face can be put on someone else's body using AI and made to look as if they are doing something they are not. AI deepfakes have been circulating among young people. A deepfake is a digitally altered photo, video, or voice recording using someone's identifying information without their permission. I share stories of my children specifically around my parenting. I am putting myself out in the world as a parent, not putting them out in the world as people. That's up to them when they are fully developed to make those decisions.

Who or what is influencing children?

Think about the term "influencer." Your children are being influenced by media, some of them for eight hours a day, seven days a week, fifty-two weeks a year. They are no longer influenced by their parents. Generation Z is dismissive of their elders, thinking they don't have anything to learn from them. Children today resist their parents' concerns and attempts to limit technology as "You just don't understand us because you're old." This is typical of younger generations to older ones, but it's different now. Children today are bombarded with media for hours a day, even while they are at school. Their level of outside influences is larger than any generation before them. If you are not influencing your child, someone else is, and they aren't influencers you want shaping your child. Children today are literally being raised on technology. Think about that. You are not raising them, tech is.

Parents, stay connected to your children. If you are connected, you will know if your child is feeling depressed, for example. If you are not connected and your child is depressed, they won't feel they can talk about it with you. Today's children have the Internet at their fingertips to get the answer to any issues they have. If a child searches for the word "depression" online because they don't feel like they can talk to their parents, the algorithm knows they are depressed. Sites such as YouTube, designed to keep the user on for as long as possible, feed depressed children self-harm videos. If they cut themselves, they won't feel the emotional pain; it's an escape, a way to control the feelings. It's quite common, and these videos are readily available in the sites' feeds. Imagine if your child talked to you before turning to an online platform. Wouldn't that be better? You can help them find healthy solutions for the way they feel.

KEY TAKEAWAYS

- ▸ Educate yourself on Big Tech's hold on our children.
- ▸ There are many ways technology is influencing young lives.
- ▸ Stay connected; when you are attuned to your children, you will be able to use your instincts.

CHAPTER 13

RECOMMENDATIONS FOR TECHNOLOGY USE

*Kids are overprotected in the real
world, and under-protected online.*
—Jonathan Haidt,
The Anxious Generation

Are we so disconnected and far away from our instincts that we can't see how technology is damaging our children? Who do we want them to be? If we want them to be strong, capable, sure of themselves, thriving adults, we need a huge wake-up call.

I once participated on a panel with a judge, a lawyer for the public schools, and a detective. The topic of the conversation was teens' digital communication and the ramifications of inappropriate messaging. Topics covered included sexting, making threats, and cyberbullying. We are talking about middle schoolers. One of the middle school principals had organized this event because she was (and still is) having to deal with so many cases of sexting and, as a mandated reporter, she had to notify authorities, law enforcement had to get involved.

Middle schoolers lack impulse control and decision-making abilities because their prefrontal cortexes aren't fully developed. The moderator asked me the same question in different forms, and my answer was always the same. The question was, "How can we talk to our teens about being responsible with social media?"

I said, "We can't, and I don't."

I talk to the parents. It's the parents' responsibility. Not a school's. Not a detective's. Not a judge's.

They wanted me to say there is a way to avoid disappointing the kids and still have them act appropriately using social media. They don't want to do the hard thing, which is to say "no." I didn't cave. I held that it's OK to make them uncomfortable, and that requires you as the adults to do the same. Society is having to bear the burden of kids who aren't ready to have devices and social media. The schools, our law enforcement resources, and the legal system are dealing with the fallout because parents aren't strong enough to say "no."

The judge on the panel, who has older kids, said he regrets giving them access to social media too early and wishes he could go back and change that. He said he had "caved" to their pressure.

The lawyer was very upset at one point and confronted me. "So you're telling me that you are going to wait to give your kid, at eighteen, access to social media, send him off to college, and say 'see ya'?" His point was that because I don't allow social media for my teenager, he won't be properly prepared for life.

To which I replied with a resounding "Yes!"

You see, he has it backward.

If you don't give children access to things they aren't ready for early on, their development proceeds naturally. They become strong, capable, independent, and self-reliant. They're able to have critical thinking, socialize, look people in the eye and talk to them, and more. I also said my son has a deep connection with us, and I trust him to manage himself because he's not scrolling mindlessly and interacting virtually with people he barely knows. He connects to us—we influence him!

That concept—giving kids technology early to teach them how to use it so when they grow up they will be ready for the world—has never made sense to me. This isn't like teaching them how to cook or do laundry. A one-year-old can learn how to use this stuff! We adults figured it out quite quickly despite not growing up with it. It's not a sound argument. In fact, not giving it to them young helps them develop in all the ways described in child development. Not giving it to them before they are ready makes them ready when they are older! Not overprotecting them in the real world allows them to be discerning online and know how to manage it later.

I told the lawyer and the audience we have the example of Gen Z to prove my point! They were given tech access too early, and they aren't doing so well. For example, 42 percent of them have a mental health diagnosis. This really solidified that my message is more important than ever! Adults must do the work on themselves to hold the space for the kids' discomfort.

For the children's own good.

Parents, we must be willing to take a stand. I know there is mounting pressure from your kids, the school, their coaches, and society. We must ask ourselves, *Are we followers or leaders?* People have come after me with pitchforks for years. I know in my heart and in my gut I am doing the right thing. I see it in my children. They are connected, emotionally intelligent humans with their feet on the ground, and they will be ready for the world when they leave the nest.

If you delay until they are older, more mature, and more responsive to your influence, then you can talk to them about how to have an appropriate relationship with tech. I ask them, "What is your relationship with technology? If you are overusing it and have too much in your life, that's the relationship you are prioritizing. Is that what you want? Or do you want strong real-life relationships? Meaningful ones?" They hear this. They appreciate being talked to this way. They are usually treated like they can't handle the truth. They absolutely can, and they need us, they want us to tell them because they know nothing else. That's our fault. We owe them.

Boundaries around tech

When I was a teenager entering high school, I asked my mom if I could go to a house party. Her first question was, "Are the parents going to be home?" I could have easily lied and said yes, but I told the truth. The parents were not going to be home. My mom said no to my request. I was relieved. The idea of going to a high school party where there would be drinking, among other things that were beyond my readiness, terrified me. I knew my mom would say no. I *wanted* her to say no because I couldn't say no myself. I wasn't mature enough to tell my friends. I think about that now in the context of children's exposure to media. They need us to set boundaries for them; the guardrails make them feel safe. They will fight it, but that's their job. Your job is to stand strong, grounded in knowing they need you to say no. You are not their friend, and it's OK to disappoint them. If you set the boundary in their childhood and protect them from harm, they will be your friend when they are adults. Put in the hard work when they are young, and long term it will pay off in your relationship.

People often ask me when I give a keynote, "What is good about technology?" My answer is, "I'm not here to talk about the good." We have allowed tech to take over our connection to self. Tech is actively seeking to fill the gaps of discomfort in our lives. Collectively, we lack boundaries with digital technology. What can parents do? We can let children be bored, entertain themselves, tolerate painful feelings, do hard things, and challenge themselves. I'm here to talk about that. That's more important to me than what's good about technology.

Remember the Big Tech executives who send their children to device-free schools? The philosophy behind this is that there is a time and place for screens. These children's parents use screens in their everyday life because they are adults and know how to have boundaries around them. Just as we wouldn't allow a child to see an R-rated movie or have an alcoholic beverage, we need to see screens this way as well. There should be a minimum age to use them. These high-tech parents feel that they did not use screens as children and therefore were able to develop their creative-thinking skills to become successful in the technology world.

The following is a list of recommendations of specific ages when technology should and should not be introduced. However, my goal in this book is to empower you to make the decisions about when to introduce tech yourselves for your children and family. Remember, I'm not the expert, you are!

Ages birth-5

I don't recommend tablets, smartphones, or even streaming TV for anyone under five years of age. This is a critical period of brain development, so parents should be cognizant of their own usage of devices during this time. Babies and toddlers need a lot of human interaction. From three to five, it's OK for them to watch movies with parents

RECOMMENDED

Ages 0–5 No tablets, smartphones, or streaming TV	**Ages 3–5** Can watch a movie as a family
Ages 5–10 Minimal usage of screens under adult supervision	**Ages 9–12** More independence in the real world, can have a safe watch
Ages 12–14 Safe device sans Internet and social media apps	**Ages 14–18** Can introduce smart devices, no social media

Source: Nicole Runyon

and virtually interface with family members far away via Zoom and Facetime.

But they should be looking at books instead of tablets. Interacting with humans in real life. Giving and receiving eye contact. Learning expressive and receptive language. For younger children, many apps have seductive music and flashing lights to gain the users' attention. These apps are peddled as educational, when they are drawing the child in for a lifetime of screen usage. They're designed to trigger the brain's pleasure response immediately and wire the brain for addiction. I see so many parents giving their babies and toddlers devices in public spaces to keep them quiet and calm. This is short-term relief that causes long-term pain. The device is priming them for addiction and stunting their growth at the same time. Think of what they are not doing by being on the device. They are not learning frustration tolerance, patience, and social interaction. If you have a toddler who is interested in the world around them and you want them to sit still in a restaurant without a device, you can bring activities for them to engage in, such as drawing, reading books, or walking around and then returning to their seat. Their attention span is short, so make sure to have some go-tos ahead of time to keep them engaged in real-world activities.

Ages 5-10

Technology should be very limited and in the form of, for example, family movie nights. This age group should have minimal exposure to a tablet, smart device, or video game system, only using it under adult supervision. Educational games are subject to ads just as any other online platform. Also, advertisers aren't required to adhere to producing content with age limits. Many parents feel safe allowing their children to play games such as Geometry Dash, yet kids are being exposed to nude ads for an AI girlfriend through that very app. Your children should not be on devices unsupervised in this age range.

Such things as YouTube tutorials are OK if viewed under supervision and if the kids connect what they learn to real-world applications. YouTube can be a slippery slope into watching recommended videos, which can be dangerous. Five- to ten-year-olds should be playing with LEGOs instead of Minecraft, and middle schoolers should be interacting with their friends in person rather than over social media and online video gaming.

Ages 9-12

Children at this age can have watches such as Gabb and Gizmo. This allows them to keep in touch with parents safely without Internet and social media access. Gabb makes safe devices that grow with the child. It's a great compromise for a parent to allow their child independence and feel they can practically stay in touch if need be. Many of us parents today had pay phones to stay in touch with our parents. Since those phones no longer exist, safe devices are an alternative to a smart device.

There is also a school of thought that says kids at this age don't need anything to stay in touch, as they should be out in the world experiencing life without supervision. I love that philosophy and think it's ideal, but I'm not a stickler if you feel you want to stay in touch. I do, however, think tracking your children at this age is fear-based and not good for their overall confidence and self-trust. Many safe devices have tracking capabilities for parents who want to know where their children are. Statistically, life outside of the home is safer for children than it was when we were growing up. Giving your children the impression that something bad is going to happen to them on their way to the park is not only inaccurate but is causing them to have anxiety about being away from you and preventing them from developing as they should. My kids had watches at these ages, and I never used location tracking. I trusted they were where they were supposed to be, and thus they trusted themselves.

Many parents feel it's OK to give a smart device at these ages with parental controls. Think twice; the children are smarter than you! They know how to get around all your parental controls. I talked to kids for years who told me all the creative ways to do so. I don't recommend parental controls. I think if you must control your child's screen time for time and content, they have no business being on a screen. They are too young and not ready to manage it. You are taking away their autonomy to make good choices because it was given to them too young.

Ages 12-14

For this age range, consider Gabb or Pinwheel, which are alternatives to full-capability smart devices. They look like a regular smartphone and children can talk and text their friends. Old-school flip phones are also an option. Also, a landline phone can be great at this age if you feel your child is not ready for texting. Many children are not ready during this time. Safe devices are designed to block inappropriate texts, but kids may still engage in conversations beyond their maturity level. You know your child. If you are going to use a device that allows texting, I suggest parents monitor those texts at this age, and these devices allow you to do so. Talk to your kids regularly about group chats and cyberbullying. Inappropriate things are said via text on a regular basis, and children need to know that what they say is permanent and will follow them. Based on child development, most middle schoolers and younger are not ready for smartphones. As I talked about earlier, the ages of eleven to fourteen are a critical time for identity development. These adolescents are too young to have boundaries with a smartphone. This is the age group where I see the most dysfunction around phones. Also, remember Piaget's stage of cognitive development. Before twelve, children are preoperational. Their minds aren't quite analytical yet. If they are exposed to content beyond their years, before their analytical brains can process it, they will internalize it. This can lead to all sorts of misinterpretation of what they saw.

Unfettered access to the Internet can lead to children seeing sexual images, dead bodies, self-harm, and violence. Children can be coerced to send predators nude photos of themselves and engage in sex acts online. Groomers are everywhere online in kids' spaces. They lure them into chat rooms where they pretend to be a child their age. They compliment them, make them comfortable, and then ask for sexual images. Groomers attempt to desensitize children to sex by talking to them about it and showing them pornographic pictures and videos. Some of them go so far as to ask a child to meet up with them. The child agrees because they were manipulated by the grooming techniques.

Many kids are being sex trafficked online under their parents' roofs. Most people think sex trafficking happens from kidnappings, but online predators are sophisticated in the way that they lure young children to meet up. An organization called United Against Human Trafficking estimates that 65 percent of victims in the US age seven to eleven are recruited from online websites and social media. Furthermore, fewer than 10 percent of cases happen due to kidnapping.[85] Sex traffickers use the dark web to hide their identities and are careful not to leave a paper trail. They are savvy and know how to gain trust with children. Signs that your child may be a victim of online trafficking include changing their appearance, sneaking out at night, and possessing extravagant gifts or extra money (one of the ways young people are lured in).

These years are a time for protection and connection. Protect them by keeping them off the Internet and social media. Connect with them by explaining the reasons why. This is a great time for teaching. Your influence is gold. Talk to them about sexting and sending nude photos. Having possession of nude photos on your device is a federal offense and is not protected under First Amendment rights because it's technically possession of child pornography. Many children in this age range are very impulsive; even armed with this information, they can't help themselves and still send and accept nude photos of one another.

Ages 14-18

The approach to technology use in this age range depends on your individual child and their maturity. If your teenager demonstrates that they are developing naturally and are well-adjusted, a smart device can be introduced—but only after you've taught them about such things as inappropriate texting, online dangers such as sextortion, and cyberbullying. Talk to them about how addictive technology can be. Have a plan for if they feel they are starting to overuse their device, stay up too late on it, or if they receive a nude or suggestive photo. This is where your connection really matters because you have to put your trust in them to the test. Have an age minimum for smartphones that makes sense for your family. If your child doesn't seem ready at fourteen, stick with a safe device until you see more maturity.

If you give your fourteen-year-old a smart device, you should still have rules and boundaries around it. I don't think anyone under eighteen should be on social media. Yes, eighteen! We have age limits for cigarettes, alcohol, marijuana, narcotic medicines, and gambling. As you've learned, there is a reason for that developmentally. The prefrontal cortex is still developing all through adolescence and young adulthood. We know the damages social media has caused our children. Why is putting an age limit on it so unbelievable? I don't think the social media bans for children should have to come from the government. I know there is legislation in some states banning the use for children. I want to empower parents to make informed choices. We don't need to wait for legislation and regulation on Big Tech. Remember, the kids are smarter than us. They will find ways around the bans and regulations. There is talk on the national scene about TikTok bans, and now Instagram has come up with a teen version. Kids will find the next app that allows them more access to what they want. It's better to foster an environment that allows them to make good choices. Create a space for them to know the facts and choose not to use a smart device.

Many people argue that kids will go behind their parents' backs and have burner phones or create accounts incognito, so we should allow them to have it. I see this the same as drugs and alcohol. Teens will be rebellious when something is forbidden. That doesn't mean we condone the behavior and tell them it's OK to use a dangerous substance. It's more reason to work on our relationships with them so they respect us enough to listen. It doesn't have to be punitive or harsh, just intentional. Technology doesn't have to be a fight between parents and children.

Have common-sense rules for your teen's smart device, and if they break the rules, you must take the device away. I know this one is difficult. Here are some more specific ideas and recommendations designed to help you navigate tech use in your family.

1. **Limit the amount of time spent on all technology.** Proceed with caution on this one. Remember the conversation about addiction?

It only takes a little bit of time for the dopamine response to occur and the child to become addicted. After you've given a child a screen, they will become angry if you take it away. The timer goes off, and there will be pushback. I have also heard from parents who limit the data on their teens' phones and tablets. When the data runs out, they are done with their phones until data is reloaded for the next month. This stands to reason. However, even when their use is limited, screens are highly addictive. It only takes one click or tap to make a child feel good. During this time teens are susceptible to social media and video games. With every "like" and comment a teen will feel pleasure and want more, even if this occurs for a half hour per day because a timer is set. It's the same with video games, which are designed to be seductive and addictive using auditory and visual stimulation.

2. **No devices at any mealtime.** This is so important. I know that many families are busy and sometimes a family dinner does not happen. If you can fit it in, please sit with your children and talk without any technology. That includes you, parents. No screens at the table. This goes beyond dinnertime. You can be honest with them about why you are placing restrictions on their phone usage. Explain to them that it's not healthy to be on their screens constantly. Social

media and smartphones have changed the culture
in a way that is detrimental to parent and child
relationships. It has disconnected us, preventing
us from having deep, meaningful conversations.
Families today are busy, and dedicated, intentional times without devices help maintain the
family connection.

3. **Check in the phone one hour before bedtime
   to allow teens to wind down.** You, too, parents.
   Again, you must model a balance with your
   devices. The light from the screen stimulates
   the brain and makes it difficult for the nervous
   system to settle. Also, exposure to blue light at
   night has been linked to depression in numerous
   studies. Teens need their sleep in order to function in their daily lives. Make sure they are not
   going to bed with their phone. They do not know
   how to shut it off at an appropriate time and
   will be on it until all hours of the early morning.
   Many teens appear "wired and tired." They are
   exhausted but cannot calm down due to the
   wired feeling they receive from the screens. Teens
   are being given ADD/ADHD diagnoses, and
   some even placed on medication, before anyone
   even understands that their lack of focus is
   directly related to being wired and tired. Many
   teens can avoid this diagnosis and medication
   altogether if given the opportunity for the
   nervous system to settle before sleep.

4. **Taking screens away is not a punishment; it's discipline.** There is a difference. They need you to have firm boundaries. It's what makes them feel safe. What I mean is *emotionally* safe, not safe from experiencing their feelings; this distinction has been lost in our culture. I have seen teens who have not learned how to interrelate with others in the real world and parents who enable that rather than take their screens away and teach them how to relate. If your child is displaying disorder, dysfunction, and/or disconnect in their lives, it's time to take the screen away. Again, I don't advocate taking the phone away as punishment for breaking a rule. That is disjointed, and the lesson gets lost on the teenager. I know it's tempting to use the phone as a form of control as kids get older and parents feel a loss of control, but ideally, parents should allow for natural consequences as a result of things a teen does or does not do wrong.

5. **Talk to your teen.** Encourage open communication constantly. Some of these topics will be uncomfortable for you and for them. Push through it. Talk about pornography, sexting, sextortion, cyberbullying, and potential threats in a group chat or on social media. Ask them how they feel about social media. Does it make them self-conscious, anxious, depressed? They will be annoyed with you for bringing it up. Let them be annoyed. In *Being 13*, a CNN special report, it was reported

that two-thirds of the parents underestimated just how lonely, depressed, and anxious their children were due to social media use. The parents weren't aware of how much conflict their teen was involved in.[86] There are ways to have a healthy relationship with your teen if they are using a screen. Open communication is very important and necessary. Talk to your teens about what is going on in their lives, so you are not part of the two-thirds. Use the strength of your relationship with your child to help them through the difficulty of being a screenager. If you bring awareness to issues such as screen addiction, they will be able to recognize it in themselves and be more likely to manage it on their own rather than having you micromanage it.

6. **What if Pandora's box is already open?** If you are a parent reading this and thinking, *Oh no, I should not have allowed tech so soon. What do I do?* I am here to tell you **it's not too late.** If your child is under fourteen, I suggest taking devices away completely. You can explain to them that you have learned some things you didn't know previously and give them age-appropriate reasons for why you are making this change. You need to know three things about this:

   - One, they will fight, yell, scream, melt down, get depressed, and be angry. It's OK. It's good. Discomfort is a sign of growth. Here's where you can apply being uncomfortable with your child's discomfort. They will beg you to reconsider. The master-negotiator kids will use all the tactics to explain why they should have the tech. Hold the space—they need you to be strong.

+ Two, extreme reactions are signs of withdrawal and can last up to several weeks in some cases. Most often, I see kids go back to homeostasis within forty-eight hours. Many parents report seeing a different kid almost immediately. They will regulate themselves with your help. I promise! You will see a different kid. Your family will be happier.

+ Three, it's not just taking the devices away; it's reconnecting as a family to replace the devices. That's the real healing in action. Spend time together as a family. This doesn't have to be a big outing. It could be running errands together, cooking meals together, doing household chores, working as a team. This will go a long way. You will get moans and groans initially, but you are showing them a more connected way. Eventually, they will feel that and the arguments will subside. I have borne witness to families doing this and it's amazing how this one change, simple but hard, calms everyone's nervous systems. You have to ask yourself what is missing for them in the real world that makes them feel they need the virtual world. Maybe they need challenges in their life to gain confidence and agency. Maybe they need to build social skills and relationships. You can help them with what is missing and feel more in control. I know that device is making you feel out of control. You can do this!

Finally, one of the most important factors is that **you as the parent need to model healthy behaviors with technology**. I know you work. So do I! But you don't have to be shopping online, scrolling on social media, watching YouTube videos, or otherwise checking out when your children are around. You can have designated tech times for the whole family. Limit it, and then do something else.

Lastly, depending on the severity of their symptoms, some teens (over fourteen) need to stop using their screens altogether and take a break for an extended period. This can be a few weeks, a few months, or longer. Specifically, if the teen is depressed, anxious, lonely, or withdrawn, a "cold turkey" approach will allow them to reflect inward and rebuild relationships that were disconnected due to the screen. Also, this approach may be appropriate if the teen is bullying others online.

This is not an easy approach. I have witnessed teens' devices taken away and parent reports of severe anger. This is a typical initial reaction, and once the teen moves past their angry reaction, a connection can be rebuilt. I have also witnessed this. Reflecting inward is such an important tool for life. The field of psychology has been turning toward an ideology called *mindfulness*. We believe that if humans take time daily to be "in" the present moment, it can reduce stress and increase happiness. It is impossible to be mindful in your life if you exist in front of a screen for most of it.

A study at UCLA showed that when children spend five days without their devices, their capacity for empathy increases.[87] This is a hopeful statistic because it shows that the emotional damage that may have occurred due to the screen can be undone. Another benefit of a break from screens is that the parent/child relationship can resume. At the middle school and high school ages, teens need independence. With the absence of a phone, that autonomy can blossom.

We must lean in to our relationships and replace screen time with people time. We must spend more quality time with our teens when they are at home, which means turning off screens. It is important to understand that a child's emotional development has not changed, and that though our culture has changed, humans still develop in the same way we always have. Let's remember what they need before blindly handing them a screen.

I hear many parents report that taking the devices away or delaying use has caused (or they fear will cause) depression, social isolation, not "fitting in," and that the damage will be worse than the device usage. I say not having the distraction builds their character and allows them to develop the skills they need. They are not missing out, they are benefitting. Parents, you are enough for your children. Your connection to them is enough! If they don't have a device because you are delaying use or you felt it was appropriate to take it away, replace it with real-life human connection.

My mom used to say, "If so and so jumped off a bridge, would you?" I know I'm not the only one who heard that growing up. This was her way of explaining to me that following my friends into something harmful was nonsensical! She was right! A common argument for allowing children to be on social media or have a device at a young age is that if we don't, they will be ostracized and left out. They won't have friends or a social life. Here's a counter-argument: Sometimes being "the only one" is a good thing. Don't follow the crowd. Be different. Isn't this what we teach our kids in general? Why is screen access any different? Do your thing. Take a stand. That's how leaders are made. It's never easy, but nothing worth doing is ever easy, and parents must be comfortable with their child's discomfort.

Not having a device or access to social media forces children and teens to figure out how to be social in real life. It teaches them independence and fosters growth. It forces them to interact with human beings. I could think of a hundred different reasons why not having a device too soon or social media at all during childhood is a good idea, but I am choosing the following example because I find it incredibly disturbing. My friend Anya was walking her dog one day when a group of college students stopped to pet the pup. Anya noticed that the girls were dressed like they had just rolled out of bed even though it was the middle of the day. She asked them, "Why are you dressed this way?" They said they dress down during the day because later, when they are done with class, they dress up in cute outfits, apply makeup, do their hair, and take selfies and videos for social media. Anya was just as astonished as I at how unbelievable it was that the girls thought the world we think is real is not real. Their reality is on social media.

If you finish reading this book with nothing else, I want you to understand that you are not powerless. We as parents can prevent our kids from suffering. We do not want to see them have anxiety, depression, and addictive behaviors. It's massively uncomfortable to go against the grain and delay usage, have rules about social media, and enforce overall limits. I believe it's the sacrifice parents need to make for their children.

Since you are reading this book, you are a well-intentioned parent who wants to see their child develop into a happy, healthy independent person. You can do this by bringing more awareness to your entire family's use of screens.

KEY TAKEAWAYS

- ▸ Giving kids and teens unfettered access to Internet and social media apps is damaging to their development.
- ▸ Boundaries around technology can help build the parent-child connection and deepen trust.
- ▸ It's up to us parents to keep our children safe, even if it's hard on us because they are different from their peers and have social consequence as a result.

Extras

If you haven't already, be sure to download the *Free to Fly Kit* by going to the website https://nicole-runyon. mykajabi.com/-bonus-material or scanning the QR code below.

There you will find a hidden bonus to help you with the chapter you just read. Simply enter your name and email to receive the kit. Then take the *What Is Your Relationship with Technology?* assessment to determine what your relationship is with digital technology. You will also find the *Activities Cheat Sheet* to be helpful here as well, so you can learn ways for your family to spend time together tech-free.

CONCLUSION

Connection is protection.
—LESLIE WEIRICH

IF YOUR FAMILY IS LIKE MOST OTHERS, YOU ARE OVER-scheduled and exhausted, leaving you checked out and scrolling on your phone during your free time and disconnected from your children. You have no idea how to find your way to connection. Think of this: Connection is simple. It's looking up from your phone, talking to a neighbor, experiencing a sense of community. We used to be tribal. Living communally, helping one another. We are so isolated on devices that we've lost a sense of support from one another.

We give and receive connection through understanding ourselves to understand our children. When you connect to yourself, you can connect to others. Connection heals. Connection is at the source of solving any problems with your children. You must do the hard work. Let yourself be uncomfortable so you can allow your children the discomfort to grow.

When I think about how connection heals, I am reminded of a teenager I saw for psychotherapy. Lorelei (not her real name) had a great connection with her therapist prior to seeing me. However, that therapist moved, and she was seeking to find someone to replace her. Lorelei presented with depression, anxiety, and suicidal ideation. During her initial therapy sessions, she displayed apathy and wasn't interested or engaged; she would often fall asleep. She showed signs of trauma and was resistant to trust me. She didn't want to get attached to another therapist only to have me leave too. Lorelei had some ACEs. She was the oldest of three, her parents were divorced, and she had taken on a caretaking role with her younger sisters. Lorelei had been sexually assaulted by a boy her age, though she didn't share that until two years into therapy with me.

At the end of one fateful therapy session her mom had come to pick her up. She was complaining about Lorelei to me in the waiting room as she was leaving my office. Lorelei wasn't responsible enough, her grades were failing, she was getting into vaping and drinking. I invited the mother into my office alone so we could discuss this. I didn't want Lorelei to hear such negativity about herself. I thought it'd be counterintuitive to our rapport building. I wanted to show her that I was willing to work with her mom, not just nod my head to her complaints and send them on their not-so-merry way.

When we were alone, I asked Lorelei's mother to be patient with her daughter's process as she worked through her issues. I told her we were on the same page; I wanted the same things she wanted for Lorelei. I wanted her to be a healthy, successful, thriving adult. I used the analogy of different roads leading to the same destination. I said I wanted to try to help her go down a different road than her mother was advocating for. Lorelei's mother wanted her to strive for excellence since she knew Lorelei was so capable. She did this by riding her and criticizing the things she wasn't doing. She didn't understand the root causes for what was happening. I didn't expect her to, but she didn't even ask. She wanted Lorelei to just do it without the healing part. It was an unrealistic expectation especially for a kid. I fully agreed with her that Lorelei was capable of excellence; all kids are. I said she could be excellent, but not by us being critical. We could push her but not yet.

The next time I saw Lorelei she said, "Thanks for trying with my mom, but it's a lost cause. She didn't like what you said."

I said, "I'm sorry."

She said, "It's OK, it's not your job."

I locked eyes with Lorelei and in a firm, serious voice said, "Yes, it is. I'll keep trying."

It was in that moment that Lorelei began healing. I connected with her in a way that no one else had. She let me in. She stopped falling asleep in her sessions, was engaged, and participated. She continued to hide things about herself but not because she wasn't comfortable with me. As I said in the early pages of this book, the therapist is a mirror. Lorelei wasn't ready to face her trauma or her reactions to the trauma. The connection with me was enough for her to try to make her life better until she was ready to thrive.

Once the connection was built and Lorelei began talking about her trauma in our therapy, I could get tough. I called this "tough love," and she tolerated it just fine! I began challenging her on why she didn't have boundaries with people in her life who didn't treat her well, her friends and boyfriends. She had a long history of problems with friends taking advantage of her kind soul. I pushed her to be uncomfortable and tell people what she wanted and needed. This was a struggle, but eventually it clicked. Lorelei was able to have enough respect for herself and her future to forge deeper, more meaningful friendships— ones that allowed her to be herself and feel taken care of and respected. Even though our therapy came to a close, Lorelei continues to check in with me from time to time. She's more in control of herself and her life. Our connection remains, even though she is no longer my psychotherapy client.

I've always been good at attunement. When I was a young therapist, I interviewed for an in-home job to work one-on-one with a boy who had autism. His mom asked me if I had multiple training certificates and I said I did not, but that I worked with children just like her son. She was apprehensive to hire me, but she did anyway. After I'd worked with him for a few weeks, she noticed I was doing the therapy based on the trainings she usually requires of therapists working with her son. She called my method by name. I can't tell you the name because I don't remember. It was insignificant to me then and still is now. I told her I was connected to her son, I cared about him deeply and wanted to help him, so I worked with him based on my connection. I have always just known what to do when it came to helping kids. The same is true for me now. I am following my instincts. Kids need strong parents. I know I am now called to help parents give their children what they need.

You are hiding, your kids are hiding, and the present is the ground between you.

Our connection to our children works the same as mine with Lorelei. We, the parents, are the mirror. Children see themselves in us, and we see ourselves in them. That's why parenting is so hard. It's a jumble of us and them. Thinking of this reminds me of a book I read years ago by Anthony Marra. The title is the medical dictionary's definition of life, *A Constellation of Vital Phenomena*. The full definition: a constellation of vital phenomena—organization, irritability, movement, growth, reproduction, adaptation.[88] Our connection lies in holding space for kids' uncomfortable feelings. Life is full of organization, irritability, movement, growth, reproduction, and adaptation. We are here to prepare them for life. They are here to learn something. If the mirror reflects that, we will be the parents our children need, and we will be enough.

I remember several times in my childhood finding my mother pensive with a somewhat worried look in her eyes. Being sensitive to other people, I would often ask her with worry in my voice, "What are you thinking about?" She would come out of deep thought, look at me, smile, and say, "I'm thinking about how much I love you." That always comforted me, but only temporarily because I didn't believe her. I knew she was only reassuring me that she was OK because she didn't want me to worry. Adult problems belong with adults and are for them to work through, not to put on children. I now know that is what parents do. We sacrifice for our children. We hold our pain and theirs; we are the container. We allow our children to experience life in all its imperfections without the weight of the world on them.

My paternal grandmother was from Lebanon. There was a term of endearment in Arabic she used to say to us grandchildren, "Ya'aburnee," which translates into English as, "You bury me." Its meaning is complex. On the surface she was telling us she wanted to die before we did because she couldn't bear to live without us. But behind that ultimate sacrifice, she was really telling us, "I love you so much, I would die for you." Parental love is that deep. Parents love their children unconditionally. I implore you to take that love and put it into practice. I would take a bullet for my kids, and today that bullet is technology's hold on them. I will stand in front of that gun and protect them forever.

If our love is that powerful, our love is enough to protect them, even from the giants. Parents, take the power back. The only way Big Tech, Big Food, and Big Pharma win is if we let them. Don't let them be in control of our children. We get to be the agents of change! I'm rallying the troops of warrior parents who will stop at nothing to protect our children.

Are you with me? Let's protect the children online and allow them to explore the real world! They will thrive. They will fly!

ACKNOWLEDGMENTS

I AM DEEPLY GRATEFUL TO MISSION DRIVEN PRESS FOR publishing this book and believing in a first-time author. AJ and Rory Vaden, Isla Lake, and Carolina Groom— your support has meant the world to me. The team at Forefront Books was instrumental in bringing this book to life. Amanda Bauch's edits made me a stronger writer, and Jennifer Gingerich at Forefront Books was a constant source of support, responding to my questions promptly and helping me navigate moments of stress and anxiety. Special thanks to Brand Builders Group, whose expertise helped me clarify my message and structure the manuscript, making the writing process smooth and enjoyable.

To everyone who contributed to the bonus materials for this book—you are rock stars! A special shout-out to my childhood best friend, Erica Breining, and her team at MD Consulting NY, especially Donna LaRocque, for your help with digital marketing. My gratitude extends to the team at E and H Productions LLC—Chris Emmerson, Maurice Hogan, and Eric Novak—for helping me with the bonus material. To my friend and colleague Sarah Emmerson, thank you for your insights during the master class. I'm also grateful to Leslie Weirich, Delia McCabe, Miriam Mandel, Anya Pechko, Lenore Skenazy, and BG Mancini, whose ideas and contributions enriched this book.

To my clients—you have honored me by trusting me with your stories and allowing me to hold space for your vulnerability. You've taught me so much about the strength of the human spirit and inspired me to work through my own challenges as I supported you in yours. To those who permitted me to include your experiences in this book, thank you for helping others connect to stories of pain and resilience.

To you, the reader—it takes tremendous courage to reflect on your parenting. I believe it's one of the hardest but most rewarding forms of self-exploration. Thank you for showing up, engaging with this book, and committing to raising confident children who will one day shape the world.

To my siblings—Michael Aubrey, Nick Aubrey, Jason Aubrey, and Natalie Adamo—you taught me the importance of empathy and connection, the foundation of my work. To my children—Oliver and Noelle—walking this parenting journey with you makes me strive to grow every day. You inspire me to be the best version of myself.

To my parents—Michael and Lorraine Aubrey—your unwavering love and sacrifices have shaped who I am today. Your encouragement when I pursued a career in psychology and your support throughout my education and parenting journey have been invaluable. This book would not exist without you.

Finally, to my husband, Douglas—you are fearless, a dreamer, and my perfect balance. This book is as much yours as it is mine. Your unwavering encouragement and willingness to shoulder responsibilities at home gave me the space to write and edit. Thank you for standing by me through every challenge and for being my true partner in life and in this project.

ENDNOTES

INTRODUCTION

1   Amanda Lenhart, "Teens, Social Media & Technology Overview 2015,"
    Pew Research Center, April 9, 2015, https://www.pewresearch.org/
    internet/2015/04/09/teens-social-media-technology-2015/.

2   Abigail Shrier, *Bad Therapy: Why the Kids Aren't Growing Up* (Sentinel,
    2024).

3   Shrier, *Bad Therapy*.

CHAPTER 1: THE MIRROR

4   Dr. John Deloney (@johndeloney), February 15, 2024, 12:27 pm, https://x.
    com/johndelony/status/1758181186201882856.

CHAPTER 2: THE FOUR PARTS OF CHILD DEVELOPMENT

5   "Inspiring Quotes on Child Learning and Development," Vince Gowmon,
    Healing for a New World, https://www.vincegowmon.com/inspiring-
    quotes-on-child-learning-and-development/.

6   John S. Hutton, MD, MS, "Screen Usage Linked to Differences in Brain
    Structure in Young Children," Cincinnati Children's, November 9, 2022,
    https://scienceblog.cincinnatichildrens.org/screen-usage-linked-to-differ-
    ences-in-brain-structure-in-young-children/.

7   Samantha Heidenreich, OTD, MOT, "Understanding Primitive Reflexes:
    How They Impact Child Development and Intervention Strategies for
    Integration," OccupationalTherapy.com, May 6, 2021, https://www.
    occupationaltherapy.com/articles/understanding-primitive-reflex-
    es-they-impact-5409-5409.

8   Happiest Baby SNOO Smart Sleeper Bassinet, Albee Baby, https://www.
    albeebaby.com/happiest-baby-snoo-smart-sleeper-bassinet.html.

9   https://www.simplypsychology.org/harlow-monkey.html.

10 "JFK Physical Fitness Statement," YouTube, 2:57 min., https://www.

youtube.com/watch?v=E0WmpszjnN8.

CHAPTER 3: FAMILY HEALTH

11 "57 Quotes on Wellness and Health to Inspire Healthy Living," Total Wellness, Employee Wellness Blog, posted by Seraine Page, January 13, 2022, https://info.totalwellnesshealth.com/blog/quotes-on-wellness-and-health.

12 "Childhood Obesity Facts," CDC, https://www.cdc.gov/obesity/childhood-obesity-facts/childhood-obesity-facts.html.

13 Michael F. Jacobson, "Big Food Sounds Like Big Tobacco," *HuffPost*, June 2, 2015, https://www.huffpost.com/entry/big-food-big-tobacco_b_7486934.

14 Tara O'Neill Hayes, Katerina Kerska, "PRIMER: Agriculture Subsidies and Their Influence on the Composition of U.S. Food Supply and Consumption," American Action Forum, November 3, 2021, https://www.americanactionforum.org/research/primer-agriculture-subsidies-and-their-influence-on-the-composition-of-u-s-food-supply-and-consumption/.

15 Casey Means, MD, "Podcast Video: How Big Pharma Keeps You Sick, and the Dark Truth About Ozempic and the Pill - Dr. Casey Means and Calley Means on The Tucker Carlson Show," August 16, 2024, CaseMeans.com, https://www.caseymeans.com/learn/podcast-tucker-carlson.

16 Haley Scheich, Tarek Pacha (@mysuperherofoods), "Who's surprised?!? ...," Instagram, September 8, 2024, https://www.instagram.com/mysuperherofoods/reel/C_rIox6Me5P/.

17 By permission.

18 By permission.

CHAPTER 4: COGNITIVE DEVELOPMENT

19 By permission.

20 Saul McLeod, PhD, "Piaget's Sensorimotor Stage of Cognitive Development," *Simply Psychology*, last updated January 24, 2024, https://www.simplypsychology.org/sensorimotor.html.

21 Dave Asprey, "What Is Junk Light and Why is it Bad for You?" TrueLight, blog, accessed October 20, 2024, https://shoptruelight.com/luna-red-lighting-solutions/junk-light/.

22 By permission.

23 By permission.

24 Matt Richtel, "A Silicon Valley School That Doesn't Compute," *New York Times*, October 22, 2011, https://www.nytimes.com/2011/10/23/technology/at-waldorf-school-in-silicon-valley-technology-can-wait.html.

25 By permission.

26 Elizabeth M. Ross, "Despite Progress, Achievement Gaps Persist During

Recovery from Pandemic," Harvard Graduate School of Education, January 31 2024, https://www.gse.harvard.edu/ideas/news/24/01/despite-progress-achievement-gaps-persist-during-recovery-pandemic.

27 By permission.

CHAPTER 5: SOCIAL EMOTIONAL DEVELOPMENT

28 Kahlil Gibran, Quotable Quote, Goodreads, https://www.goodreads.com/quotes/197442-if-you-love-somebody-let-them-go-for-if-they.

29 Sam McLeod, PhD, "Erik Erikson's Stages of Psychosocial Development," Simply Psychology, updated on January 25, 2024, https://www.simplypsychology.org/erik-erikson.html.

30 McLeod, "Erik Erikson's Stages."

31 "The 'Still Face' Experiment by Dr. Ed Tronick," UMass Chan Medical School Psychiatry Department, YouTube, July 11, 2022, https://www.youtube.com/watch?v=FaiXi8KyzOQ.

32 Office of the Surgeon General (OSG), *Parents Under Pressure: The U.S. Surgeon General's Advisory on the Mental Health & Well-Being of Parents* [Internet], Washington, DC (US Department of Health and Human Services, 2024): 1, "The Current State of Parental Stress & Well-Being," https://www.ncbi.nlm.nih.gov/books/NBK606662/.

33 "Anxiety and Depression in Children," Centers for Disease Control and Prevention, last updated August 19, 2024, https://www.cdc.gov/children-mental-health/about/about-anxiety-and-depression-in-children.html.

34 McLeod, "Erik Erikson's Stages."

35 McLeod, "Erik Erikson's Stages."

CHAPTER 6: GENDER DYSPHORIA

36 Robin Respaut, Chad Terhune, "Putting Numbers on the Rise in Children Seeking Gender Care," Reuters, October 6, 2022, https://www.reuters.com/investigates/special-report/usa-transyouth-data/.

37 "Sex Reassignment Surgery Market Size & Share, by Gender Transition (Female-to-Male, Male-to-Female); Procedures; End-Use Global Supply & Demand Analysis, Growth Forecast, Statistics Report 2025-2037," Research Nester, November 15, 2024, https://www.researchnester.com/reports/sex-reassignment-surgery-market/6222#:~:text=The%20market%20size%20for%20sex,i.e.%2C%20between%202024%2D2036.

38 "Dilation After Gender-Affirming Surgery," Mayo Clinic, July 17, 2021, video, https://www.mayoclinic.org/vid-20517182.

39 Janella Hudson et al., "Fertility Counseling for Transgender AYAs," *Clinical Practice in Pediatric Psychology* vol. 6, 1 (2018): 84–92, https://www.ncbi.

nlm.nih.gov/pmc/articles/PMC5979264/.

40   "What to Know About Gender-Affirming Hormone Therapy," Alto Pharmacy, blog, August 24, 2021, https://www.alto.com/blog/post/transgender-hormone-therapy-side-effects.

41   Nyein Chan Swe et al., "The effects of Gender-Affirming Hormone Therapy on Cardiovascular and Skeletal Health: A Literature Review," *Metabolism Open* vol. 13, March 3, 2022, https://www.ncbi.nlm.nih.gov/pmc/articles/PMC8907681/.

42   Elizabeth Hisle-Gorman et al., "Gender Dysphoria in Children with Autism Spectrum Disorder," *LGBT Health* vol. 6, 3 (2019): 95–100, https://pubmed.ncbi.nlm.nih.gov/30920347/.

43   Janice Turner, "What Went Wrong at the Tavistock Clinic for Trans Teenagers?," Society for Evidence Based Gender Medicine, July 1, 2022, https://segm.org/GIDS-puberty-blockers-minors-the-times-special-report.

44   Jamie Phillips, "More than 1,000 children were given puberty blockers at controversial Tavistock gender clinic 'in scandal compared to doping of East German athletes', New Book Claims," *Daily Mail*, February 12, 2023, https://www.dailymail.co.uk/news/article-11741849/More-1-000-children-given-puberty-blockers-controversial-Tavistock-gender-clinic.html.

45   Tim Gruber, "A Generation of American Men Give Up on College: 'I Just Feel Lost'," *Wall Street Journal*, September 6, 2021, https://www.wsj.com/articles/college-university-fall-higher-education-men-women-enrollment-admissions-back-to-school-11630948233.

46   Matthew F. Garnett, MPH, et al., "Suicide Mortality in the United States, 2000–2020," CDC National Center for Health Statistics, NCHS Data Brief No. 433, March 2022, https://www.cdc.gov/nchs/products/databriefs/db433.htm#:~:text=The%20suicide%20rate%20for%20females,during%20the%202000%E2%80%932020%20period.

CHAPTER 7: PORNOGRAPHY

47   Exodus Cry, Facebook post, October 7, 2021, https://www.facebook.com/photo.php?fbid=10158555845647759&id=10683277758&set=a.132648242758.

48   David Greene, host, "Social Media And Teenage Girls: Not Your Mother's Adolescence," author interview with Nancy Jo Sales, NPR, February 25, 2016, https://www.npr.org/2016/02/25/468070389/social-media-and-teenage-girls-it-s-not-your-mother-s-adolescence.

49   "Kids as Young as 7 are Looking at Porn, This Study Shows," Fight the New Drug, https://fightthenewdrug.org/parents-this-study-shows-kids-as-young-as-7-are-accessing-porn/.

50 Laila Mickelwait, "How I Forced Pornhub to Take Down Child Abuse Videos," *The Times* and *The Sunday Times Magazine*, August 24, 2024, https://lailamickelwait.com/how-i-forced-pornhub-to-take-down-child-abuse-videos-the-times-and-the-sunday-times-magazine-august-24-20204/.

CHAPTER 8: CONNECTION TO SELF

51 Rudolf Steiner, QuoteFancy, https://quotefancy.com/quote/1427955/Rudolf-Steiner-Receive-the-children-in-reverence-educate-them-in-love-and-send-them-forth.

52 Waldorf Education, Association of Waldorf Schools of North America, https://www.waldorfeducation.org/waldorf-education/rudolf-steiner-the-history-of-waldorf-education.

53 Lenore Skenazy, "Why I Let My 9-Year-Old Ride the Subway Alone," *The New York Sun*, updated February 10, 2022, https://www.nysun.com/article/opinion-why-i-let-my-9-year-old-ride-subway-alone.

54 Jonathan Haidt, *The Anxious Generation: How the Great Rewiring of Childhood Is Causing an Epidemic of Mental Illness* (Penguin, 2024).

CHAPTER 9: ALLOWING FOR DISCOMFORT

55 Kirsten Weir, "Worrying trends in U.S. suicide rates," American Psychological Association, March 2019, Vol. 50, No. 3, https://www.apa.org/monitor/2019/03/trends-suicide.

56 Jean Twenge, "Has the Smartphone Destroyed a Generation?" NowComment, https://nowcomment.com/documents/235254.

57 Leslie Hope (@leslies_hope), Instagram, August 29, 2022, https://www.instagram.com/leslies_hope/p/Ch3MyI7NzqX/?img_index=1.

58 "Drug Use Among Youth: Facts & Statistics," National Center for Drug Abuse Statistics, https://drugabusestatistics.org/teen-drug-use/.

59 Sabrina Moreno, "Youth Mental Health Crisis Is Overwhelming ERs," Axios, August 16, 2023, https://www.axios.com/2023/08/16/youth-mental-health-crisis-emergency.

60 Moreno, "Youth Mental Health Crisis Is Overwhelming ERs."

61 Sareen Habeshian, "Study: Mental Health-Related ER Visits Among Young People Nearly Doubled in a Decade," Axios, May 4, 2023, https://www.axios.com/2023/05/04/mental-health-emergency-visits-youth-study.

62 "'We are having an attendance crisis as a country': Chronic absences double nationwide since COVID-19 pandemic," *CBS Mornings*, June 7, 2022, https://www.cbsnews.com/news/chronic-absences-pandemic/.

63 By permission.

64 "NAMI Chicago And Young Invincibles Applaud Gov. Pritzker's Call to Fund Campus Mental Health Services; More Funding Is Needed," Young

Invincibles, press release, February 22, 2024, https://younginvincibles. org/nami-chicago-and-young-invincibles-applaud-gov-pritzkers-call- to-fund-campus-mental-health-services-more-funding-is-needed/#:~:- text=In%20the%20annual%20survey%2C%20which,the%20survey's%20 15%2Dyear%20tenure.

65 "David Goggins: How to Build Immense Inner Strength," Huberman Lab, video, January 1, 2024, https://www.hubermanlab.com/episode/david-gog- gins-how-to-build-immense-inner-strength.

CHAPTER 10: GENERATIONAL DIFFERENCES

66 https://seleni.org/advice-support/2018/3/14/the-gift-of-the-good- enough-mother.

67 By permission.

68 "Breaking Down Divorce Rates by Generation," Goldberg Jones, August 27, 2024, https://www.goldbergjones-wa.com/divorce/divorce-by-generation/.

69 Alicia Adamczyk, "'Gray' divorce is sky-rocketing among baby boomers. It can wreak havoc on their retirements," Yahoo! Finance, May 7, 2024, https://finance.yahoo.com/news/gray-divorce-sky- rocketing-among-150221288.html.

70 Joel A. Muraco et al., "Baumrind's Parenting Styles," Press Books (2020), https://iastate.pressbooks.pub/parentingfamilydiversity/chapter/chapter- 1-2/.

CHAPTER 11: THE FAMILY SYSTEM

71 https://www.allforkids.org/news/blog/a-fathers-impact-on-child- development/.

CHAPTER 12: BIG TECH

72 Gabrielle M. Etzel, "Anxious Generation researcher says smartphones and helicopter parents are worsening youth mental health," *Washington Examiner*, April 9, 2024, https://www.washingtonexaminer.com/ policy/healthcare/2955243/anxious-generation-researcher-says-smart- phones-and-helicopter-parents-are-worsening-youth-mental-health/.

73 Stuart Wolpert, "The Teenage Brain on Social Media," UCLA Newsroom, May 31, 2016, https://newsroom.ucla.edu/releases/the-teenage-brain-on- social-media.

74 Amy Racines, "The Brain Chemistry Behind Tolerance and Withdrawal," United States Drug Testing Laboratories, Inc., blog, https://www.usdtl. com/blog/the-brain-chemistry-behind-tolerance-and-withdrawal#:~:- text=If%20the%20body%20is%20producing,imbalance%20of%20the%20

body's%20neurotransmitters.

75   Jean Twenge, *iGen: Why Today's Super-Connected Kids Are Growing Up Less Rebellious, More Tolerant, Less Happy—and Completely Unprepared for Adulthood—and What That Means for the Rest of Us* (Atria, 2017).

76   Liz Mineo, "Harvard Study, Almost 80 Years Old, Has Proved That Embracing Community Helps Us Live Longer, and Be Happier," *The Harvard Gazette*, April 11, 2017, https://news.harvard.edu/gazette/story/2017/04/over-nearly-80-years-harvard-study-has-been-showing-how-to-live-a-healthy-and-happy-life/.

77   Harvard Study of Adult Development, Harvard Medical School, 2015, https://www.adultdevelopmentstudy.org/.

78   "Our Epidemic of Loneliness and Isolation: The U.S. Surgeon General's Advisory on the Healing Effects of Social Connection and Community," Office of the U.S. Surgeon General, 2023, https://www.hhs.gov/sites/default/files/surgeon-general-social-connection-advisory.pdf.

79   "WATCH LIVE: Senate Judiciary hearing on protecting kids online," *PBS News Hour*, YouTube, https://www.youtube.com/watch?v=5gXUa_IsBpA.

80   Laura Markham, PhD, "Twelve Year Old's Backtalk," Peaceful Parent, Happy Kids, blog, https://www.peacefulparenthappykids.com/read/twelve-year-olds-backtalk.

81   "UNESCO calls for a ban on phones in schools. Here's why," World Economic Forum, August 4, 2023, https://www.weforum.org/stories/2023/08/online-learning-digital-divide-mobile-phone-school-education/.

82   Jongseok Ahn, "Exploring the Negative and Gap-Widening Effects of EdTech on Young Children's Learning Achievement: Evidence from a Longitudinal Dataset of Children in American K-3 Classrooms," *International Journal of Environmental Research and Public Health* vol. 19 (April 29, 2022), https://www.ncbi.nlm.nih.gov/pmc/articles/PMC9104322/.

83   Delia McCabe (@deliamccabe), "Our Brain Could Be Our Worst Enemy Today (Part 1)," The State of the Modern Mind, May 10, 2024, Substack, https://substack.com/@deliamccabe/p-143752661.

84   David J. Kramer, "Cyberbullying and Suicide: Who Is Responsible?", The David J. Kramer Law Firm, blog, https://www.novilaw.com/2017/08/cyberbullying-suicide/.

CHAPTER 13: RECOMMENDATIONS FOR TECHNOLOGY USE

85   Emma Waters, "U.S. Is a Top Destination for Child Sex Trafficking, and It's Happening in Your Community," The Heritage Foundation, July 27, 2023, https://www.heritage.org/crime-and-justice/commentary/

us-top-destination-child-sex-trafficking-and-its-happening-your#:~:-
text=One%20organization%2C%20United%20Against%20
Human,played%20over%20and%20over%20again.

86   Marion K. Underwood and Robert W. Faris, "Being 13: Perils of lurking
     on social media," CNN, updated October 6, 2015, https://www.cnn.
     com/2015/10/05/opinions/underwood-faris-being-thirteen-lurking-so-
     cial-media/index.html.

CONCLUSION

87   Stuart Wolpert, "The teenage brain on social media," UCLA Newsroom,
     May 31, 2016, https://newsroom.ucla.edu/releases/the-teenage-brain-on-
     social-media.

88   *The American Heritage® Medical Dictionary*. s.v. "Definition of life," retrieved
     October 23, 2024, https://medical-dictionary.thefreedictionary.com/
     Definition+of+life.